Selected Poetry of Delmira Agustini

Selected Poetry of Delmira Agustini

Poetics of Eros

EDITED AND TRANSLATED BY

Alejandro Cáceres

WITH A FOREWORD BY

Willis Barnstone

SOUTHERN ILLINOIS UNIVERSITY PRESS / CARBONDALE

18   17   16   15   5   4   3   2

Frontispiece: Delmira Agustini ca. 1907. Courtesy of the National Library
of Uruguay, Raúl Vallarino, Director. Photo of image by Daniel Mesa.

Library of Congress Cataloging-in-Publication Data
Agustini, Delmira, 1886–1914.
    [Poems. English & Spanish. Selections]
    Selected poetry of Delmira Agustini : poetics of Eros /
edited and translated by Alejandro Cáceres ; with a foreword
by Willis Barnstone.
    p. cm.
    Includes bibliographical references.
1. Agustini, Delmira, 1886–1914—Translations into English.
I. Cáceres, Alejandro. II. Title.
PQ8519.A5A23 2003
861´.62—dc21
ISBN 0-8093-2537-3 (alk. paper)   2003050394

The paper used in this publication meets the minimum requirements of
American National Standard for Information Sciences—Permanence of Paper
for Printed Library Materials, ANSI Z39.48-1992. ∞

To my mother, Carmen Ana,
in memoriam

Contents

De *Los astros del abismo* (1924)

From *The Stars of the Abyss* (1924)

Foreword: *A Poet of Life Who Prefigures the Future in Poetry Denied Her by Two Bullets*

The twentieth century has seen so many of its major poets find early death as a result of suicide, or by execution in totalitarian regimes. At age thirty-two, Hart Crane jumped from the Mexican ship *Orizaba* on his return to the States, Sylvia Plath turned on the gas in London, Miguel Hernádez died in his prison cell of tuberculosis contracted in Franco's prisons. Hernádez's death followed that of Federico García Lorca, executed at the Well of Tears outside Granada in the first days of the Spanish civil war. In Paris the leading postwar poet in the German language, Paul Celan, waded into the Seine in despair and madness. One of the great French surrealists, Robert Desnos, died of typhus at Buchenwald one day after its liberation. The inventor of surrealism, Guillaume Apollinaire, the day after Armistice Day, 1918, succumbed to a head wound he had suffered earlier in battle. In Moscow, alerted to a gang of jeerers who were to invade his reading, Vladmir Mayakovsky played Russian roulette until he lost. Earlier, Sergey Yesenin wrote his suicide note in his own blood. In internal exile in Elabuga, harassed and destitute, Marina Tsvetayeva hanged herself. In the same circle of the silenced Akhamatova and Pasternak, the great classical poet of silences, Osip Mandelshtam, disappeared in 1938 in the snows of a Soviet concentration camp. In Italy the searing novelist and poet Cesare Pavese put a pistol to his head. It would seem that suicide and execution have decimated the poetic talent of our (twentieth) century.

In the apparently unique case of Delmira Agustini, the lords of the detective mystery intervened to remove her from her genius by domestic murder, a bullet from her husband's revolver. She was only twenty-seven. Her life and poetry had been as daring and outrageous as her film noir death. Absurd seconds of who-knows-what awful fate determined that she would foreshadow the history of Latin American poetry but be deprived of a long life of poetic development. Only Albert Camus's absurd death—in a car accident in which he was merely a passenger—seems as unnecessary and tragic as was that of Delmira Agustini.

What was the life in poetry she had? She tells us through her diamond-cutting diction: "Fantasy / Wears a rare gown filled with precious stones" ("The Poet Weighs the Anchor"). Her pathos is revealed, even when she pities an inert but very much alive statue, with words that are a battle of oppositions: "Poorer than a worm, forever calm!" ("The Statue"). Here, as did Baudelaire, she sees the noble in the miserable, in this instance, a statute deprived of consciousness.

When Agustini speaks of love, she leaves no question about the sexual fire she dares make explicit—in her time almost unthinkable: "your golden key sang in my lock" ("The Intruder"). On the pillow, she writes, "Your impudence fascinated me and I adored your madness" ("The Intruder"). There is no passive woman here, waiting for her lover's announcements. She is her own person and writes what she feels, what she knows, what she wants to tell the world. And how beautifully she does so. In poem after poem, we find mysterious lines of interior illumination as in "Your figure was a stain of light and whiteness" ("The Intruder").

Delmira Agustini fell silent in 1914. Already Braque and Picasso had invented cubism in Collioure in the winter of 1909–10), but throughout Europe and America the modern diction, in poetry of the twentieth century had not taken hold. It begins in young Antonio Machado, in Jules Laforgue, in early William Carlos Williams. Only in Apollinaire in France and Constantine Cavafy in Alexandria do we find full-blown modernity in enduring maturity. In Agustini we see a transition figure. She has the swans of marble but also the candor of the pillow. Her mythological references are predictably of her time, yet almost always subverted by a lexicon that will wander astonishingly elsewhere. She wrote with the love speech of an Edna St. Vincent Millay, with similar candor and courage, but Millay never changed. In the case of Agustini, I think it indisputable that she would have been charged by later twentieth-century innovations, as were Elizabeth Bishop and Marianne Moore, whose lives mark a history of modern American poetry. But she Delmira is what we have: her fragile white book, her morning songs, her empty chalices, and her stars in the abyss. Even so, she had time to experiment with prose poems and a lexicon of steel emotions that only find a precursor in seventeenth-century Sor Juan Inés de la Cruz. That is a lot and allows us to sharpen our gaze on this substantial spring and winter of a young poet. We need not look through thousands of pages to find black pearls. In her pages they shine with rays of darkness. Yet we must be careful. With a single line from her brief life, like a fated Russian heroine, she can destroy us: "With one kiss we became old" (At a Distance . . .").

Alejandro Cáceres has made a fine selection and enlightened translation of Agustini's oeuvre and, in addition, presents us with the key details of her life along with a profound and scholarly discourse on the significance of her work in the context of contemporary literary movements. His devotion to detail and concept is revealed on each page. His study is essential in making this introduction of Agustini to the reader in English felicitous.

—*Willis Barnstone*
OAKLAND

Preface

My critical edition of Delmira Agustini's complete poetry was published in 1999. This project started during the early 1980s, when I was still a student at Indiana University in Bloomington, where I had taken a course in which we analyzed, among other works, the poetry of "the five great ones of the south": María Eugenia Vaz Ferreira (Uruguay, 1880–1925), Delmira Agustini (Uruguay, 1886–1914), Gabriela Mistral (Chile, 1889–1957), Alfonsina Storni (Argentina, 1892–1938), and Juana de Ibarbourou (Uruguay, 1895–1979). Delmira Agustini, in particular, attracted my attention for her sensuous poetic voice and daring message. Of course, her poetry was not new to me at the time, but that new reading of the poet left a mark on me. During the following summer, I started collecting a bibliography and organizing a file on her. And this I continued to do for a number of years whenever I had some time to devote to this project. In the meantime, I became very involved with the writing of my dissertation on another author, and therefore the project was suspended for over two years. When I had the opportunity in 1992 to live in Montevideo for over a year and a half, however, I started working at the Agustini archives, at the Biblioteca Nacional del Uruguay; my in-depth research on the poet's work grew to fill not only that year and a half but also the following five summers. The result was a critical edition that included a detailed monograph on each work she wrote and a study of the most relevant criticism written on Agustini since 1914.

The idea of translating the poetry of Delmira Agustini started a few years ago when I felt the need to present some samples of her poetry to English-speaking audiences, in order to illustrate my arguments or points in various conference papers or lectures. The more familiar I became with her work, the more in tune with her discourse, and the more enchanted with her message, the more I realized that English-speaking audiences in general, and those involved in areas such as feminist studies, gender studies, and women studies in particular, could benefit a great deal from an English translation of Delmira Agustini's poetry. I did not realize, however, just how difficult and challenging it is to translate poetry, particularly if one wants to preserve as much as possible the original spirit of the poem. Sometimes I spent hours, days, and even weeks without finding exactly what I wanted. Other times, it came to me rather quickly. What I do know is that the relationship I was establishing with Delmira Agustini was becoming something fairly obsessive.

At a certain point, I decided I needed to try her out in public by organizing a poetry reading of my translations to see how her poetry would be received by an English-speaking audience. For that occasion, I invited a female graduate student, Jill Hildebrandt, from the Department of Mass Communication at Southern Illinois University Carbondale, to help me give a recital, in which we alternated reading my translations of some of Agustini's most celebrated poems. Poet-in-residence Allison Joseph and Jon Tribble, editor of the *Crab Orchard Review,* were in the audience; at the end of the performance, they expressed their interest in publishing five of my translations in the next issue of the journal. It was at that moment that I sensed a new opportunity for Delmira Agustini. I was happy and proud, for she had survived the test of my translations. Now, the publication of this volume marks the end of my efforts, but the beginning for the poet, now resurrected in a different language 117 years after her birth.

Works of literature are traditionally translated into the native language of the translator, and therefore such an approach was my original plan. However, I soon realized that this approach would have probably meant subjecting Agustini's poetry to reinterpretation by the translator, a result that would have been in opposition to my wish to present her work to her new audience in a more neutral fashion. While I am not opposed to new poetic creations and reinterpretations based upon the poet's manuscripts, I do believe that when a comprehensive collection of her work is offered in English for the first time, though the translations should certainly be poetic, it is most important that the translations be as literal as possible, that they should try as much as possible to respect the original works. And thus, though I never intended to undertake such a daunting project as translating these poems on my own, I had found a new solution for Agustini, as well as a new problem for myself!

My pleasant burden was eased by the research grant I was awarded by SIUC's Office of Research Development and Administration and the agreement of Darren Haney, a then-graduate student in our Spanish program, to be my research assistant and translation consultant. Darren and I worked together for two and a half years. Being a native speaker of English, with fluency in Spanish and a B.A. in classics, Darren turned out to be an invaluable help, overseeing the translation process, making sure the result was as meaningful in English as the source was in Spanish.

In this bilingual anthology, I have selected about half of the 130 poems Delmira Agustini wrote. This has allowed me to choose a number of poems from each of the books she published during her lifetime; the order in which they appear in this volume is the chronological order in which they were published. I have also included several poems from her posthumous work, *The Stars of the Abyss* (Los astros del abismo); this group includes those poems that form the cycle "The Rosary of Eros" (El rosario de Eros) and a selection of other poems included in that publication. The selection in the current volume includes all the best poems Delmira Agustini wrote, and they represent the universally accepted canon of Agustini's poetry. However, I have also included other poems that serve to trace the poet's development in her search for her poetic inner voice.

This anthology represents an homage I feel most honored to pay to an extraordinary poet and a superb woman, Delmira Agustini, whose poetic discourse can now be read for the first time in a language other than her own.

Acknowledgments

I wish to express my gratitude to the following people, whose generous help made this book possible: Professor Josep Miquel Sobrer, for his advice to me that I translate these extraordinary poems into English, my second language, and for his faith in my ability to do so; Distinguished Professor Emeritus Willis Barnstone, for his input regarding the translations; Mr. Darren W. Haney, who assisted me as a translation consultant; Professor Frederick Betz, whose suggestions regarding the introduction of the book were most helpful and insightful; Professor Edward Brunner, whose unwavering support from the early stages of this project gave me courage to continue; Dr. Karl Kageff, executive editor at Southern Illinois University Press, for his enthusiastic and constant support from our first discussions about the publication of this project and then for his specific and detailed comments on the final typescript; Professor Allison Joseph and Mr. Jon Tribble, who invited me to publish five of my translations in the *Crab Orchard Review* in the spring of 1999; Ms. Carmen Pittaluga Armán and Ms. Myriam Pittaluga Armán, for the translation into Spanish of the poem written originally in French, which opens *The Empty Chalices* (1913); and finally, Ms. Kathleen Kageff, project editor and copyeditor for the book, whose sensitive and thoughtful editorial input has not only impressed me but has also given the book a higher level of clarity and precision. To all of them, again, my most sincere thanks.

Selected Poetry of Delmira Agustini

 *Introduction*

Delmira Agustini was born in Montevideo, Uruguay, on October 24, 1886.
A descendant of Italians on her father's side and of Germans on her mother's,
she was born into a well-to-do family in the Montevidean society of the 1900s.
Agustini wrote three books of poems within a period of six years: *The White
Book (Fragile)* (El libro blanco [Frágil]), written during the years of adoles-
cence and early adulthood and published in 1907 when the poet was twenty-
one years old; *Morning Songs* (Cantos de la mañana), published in 1910; and
The Empty Chalices (Los cálices vacíos), published in 1913.[1] There is also a
fourth volume of poetry titled *The Stars of the Abyss* (Los astros del abismo),
published posthumously in 1924. The circumstances of her death, which
occurred on July 6, 1914, when the poet was twenty-seven years old, are still
surrounded by mystery, though the facts of her death are well known: Her
husband Enrique Job Reyes shot her to death with two bullets to the head and
then shot himself with two more bullets to his head.[2] However, it is not
precisely clear whether this apparent murder could not have been perhaps the
result of a suicide pact between the two. One of Agustini's early poems,
"Intimate" (Intima), suggests that possibility:

> Ah! tú sabrás mi amor, mas vamos lejos
> A través de la noche florecida;
> Acá lo humano asusta, acá se oye,
> Se ve, se siente, sin cesar la vida.
>
> Vamos más lejos en la noche, vamos
> Donde ni un eco repercuta en mí,
> Como una flor nocturna alla en la sombra
> Yo abriré dulcemente para ti
>
> Ah! you will know my love; but let us go now,
> Far away, through the blossoming night;
> Here what is human frightens, here one can
> Hear, can see, can feel unceasing life.
>
> Let us go father away into the night, let us go
> Where no echo can rebound in me,
> Like a nightly flower here in the shadow
> I shall softly open for you

Reyes and Agustini had been married for only one month and twenty-two days when she left her husband and returned to her parents' home, pronouncing the cryptic phrase, "I cannot stand so much vulgarity," which is all the more strange, since, after she had filed for divorce and while the divorce was in progress, Delmira and Enrique Job continued meeting as lovers in a humble room in a boarding house to which he had moved.[3] Agustini's biography may or may not be considered of great importance for the evaluation of her work, but it is indeed important to note that all her actions seem to have something in common: passion.

While Uruguay has traditionally been known for its democratic system, high level of education, low index of illiteracy, and prominent intellectuals and scholars in the humanities, the sciences, and the social sciences, as well as artists in all disciplines, the message Delmira Agustini was presenting to the Uruguayan society of the turn of the century was neither understood by all people nor accepted. In 1900, Montevidean society was going through a process of profound change that contributed to shaping its future in very progressive ways. The president of the country was Don José Batlle y Ordóñez, a liberal politician, whose administrations (1903–1907 and 1911–1915) brought about a dramatic and beneficial change. Nevertheless, Uruguay was traditionally a Catholic society,[4] and for many people of strong religious feelings and strict moral standards, Delmira Agustini's poetic discourse was simply too advanced, too sacrilegious, and too transgressive. Agustini's poetry focuses primarily on praising the beauty of love and the beauty of the male. Invoking Eros, the Greek god of love, she sings:

> ¡Así tendida soy un surco ardiente,
> Donde puede nutrirse la simiente,
> De otra Estirpe sublimemente loca!

> Thus lying I am an ardent furrow
> Where can be nurtured the seed
> Of another lineage sublimely mad!

From "Another Lineage" (Otra estirpe) in *The White Book (Fragile)* of 1907, these lines clearly illustrate the kind of erotic discourse and sexual aesthetics that characterize Agustini's whole work.

Nevertheless, the disdain many felt and the indignation of the religious women of society were not necessarily always observed behind closed doors. In a magnificent essay on what he called "Modesty and Flirting" (El pudor, la cachondez), Julio Herrera y Reissig, born to a distinguished family of the Uruguayan patriciate, and a well known leading figure of Uruguayan *modernismo*,[5] exposes in a blunt and sarcastic manner the hypocrisy associated with women's sexual practices in the Montevidean society of the 1900s.[6] This essay, originally a chapter of a larger essay titled "The New Charrúas" (Los nuevos charrúas), makes reference—in a most disrespectful, mordant, and ironic tone—to the women who pretended to live in society as role models of virtue and decency, while in their private lives they were intensely sexually driven and eager to experience the product of their fantasies.[7] This kind of model is common in societies highly influenced by religious beliefs and social codes of pretended decency—as in, for example, England in the nineteenth century. What matters in this case is that Delmira Agustini carried out a message both in her life and her work that her contemporaries in Uruguay were not able, much less ready, to receive.

From as early as 1903, when the first poems written by Agustini appeared in literary magazines, until the most mature poems written around 1913, the work of Agustini shows the ways in which she was developing and maturing both as a poet and as a human being, experimenting with both content and form and identifying her own lyric inner voice. Her development can be measured in an ascending line that goes from the early *modernista* sonnets, charged with the traditions of oriental palaces, exotic perfumes, and wandering princesses, to the most hermetic collection of poems she conceived towards the end of her life: *The Rosary of Eros* (El rosario de Eros), which first appeared as a posthumous work.[8]

Delmira Agustini's poetry is filled with a variety of elements that appear recurrently from *The White Book (Fragile)* of 1907 to *The Stars of the Abyss* of 1924. These elements are also commonly found in other aesthetic movements of the second half of the nineteenth century, particularly in France. For example, from the French Parnassians, such as Leconte de Lisle, Sully Prudhomme, José María de Heredia, and Charles Baudelaire, Agustini draws her cult of form and harmony, which suggests classical grandeur. On the other hand, from the French romantics, such as Victor Hugo, Alfred de Musset, and

Alphonse de Lamartine, she draws the sonority of the words and the intimacy and sentiment of the verse. From the French symbolists, such as Stéphane Mallarmé, Paul Verlaine, and Albert Samain, Agustini also draws the musicality of the verse as well as the vagueness and the intangible atmosphere of their poems. Characteristics of late-nineteenth-century decadence, also derived from French symbolism (from such poets as Verlaine, Mallarmé, and Baudelaire) can also be found in Agustini's discourse: an exaggerated refinement of the words, abnormality, perversity, exquisiteness, rareness, and exotic sensations, experienced and expressed by the hero of decadence who is consumed by the *mal du siècle*.

All these literary movements and poetic trends of the turn of the century, suggesting a constant aesthetic revolution, would be contained in the new *modernista* movement, the theory of which has been subjected to sustained discussion and revision by twentieth century scholars.

Spanish-American *modernismo* is a literary movement that started during the nineteenth century, near 1870, and lasted approximately until the second decade, around 1920, of the twentieth century; on the other hand, Anglo-American or Anglo-European modernism started later in the nineteenth century, towards 1890 in France, and lasted until the 1940s. In other European countries, as well as in America, the movement existed within a similar time span.

While for Anglo-European modernism, the term pertains to all the creative arts, particularly poetry, drama, fiction, as well as painting, music and architecture, for Spanish American *modernismo*, the term pertains to poetry and fiction. Some of the most influential modernist writers tried some radical experiments with form: poets like Pound and Eliot working in free verse, for instance, and novelists like Joyce, Woolf, and Stein experimenting with "stream of consciousness" to try to capture a character's internal thought processes. Characteristics of Anglo-European and Anglo-American modernism are often associated with or contained in other "isms" of the time, such as constructivism, dadaism, decadence, existentialism, expressionism, free verse, futurism, imagism, new humanism, symbol and symbolism, ultraism, vorticism, as well as free verse and stream of consciousness mentioned above.

As for Spanish America, the traditional vision of *modernismo* as a literary movement was one of a trend more concerned with form than content that aimed to break with the pathos and excesses brought by romanticism. This vision, which characterized the first decades of the last century, has been reevaluated during the second part of the twentieth century by a variety of scholars who consider that the political scene, the socioeconomic and philosophical changes that occurred in Latin America at the turn of the nineteenth to the twentieth century, and the relation of all these aspects to the birth of nations constitute major components of the movement. Involving both political and linguistic issues, *modernismo* is the entire experience of Spanish America entering modernity.

As early as 1962, Luis Monguió discusses the concept of "cosmopolitanism" as one of the main characteristics of *modernismo:*[9] "Around 1870 and 1880, Spanish-America . . . was going from the era of romantic nationalism, whether it was liberal or conservative, to the era of materialistic positivism" (85). Spanish American writers of the time, led by Rubén Darío, did not like the kind of materialism prevailing in their countries and felt they had to preserve beauty and idealism from the ugliness and materialistic atmosphere of daily life. In other words, "since they did not like the real world that surrounded them, they were as much cosmopolitans in their ideal world as their country-men were in the world of money" (85). However, the Spanish American War in 1898 and American construction of the Panama Canal beginning in 1903 made these writers fearful of American imperialism, which could put their national identities in danger, and therefore they felt the need to reaffirm the spiritual values in their language, nationality, religion, and tradition.[10] Or, as Cathy Jrade notes,

> the Spanish American writers of the end of the nineteenth century—most of whom lived in the urban capitals of their countries and/or traveled extensively in Europe—believed that they were confronting, in a noble struggle, the most acute issues of modern life. (2)[11]

Matei Calinescu addresses this struggle in terms of what he calls "the two modernities." He points out the impossibility of saying precisely "when one can begin to speak of the existence of two distinct and bitterly conflicting modernities" (41). Calinescu believes that at some point during the first half of the nineteenth century an irreversible split occurred between modernity as a stage in the history of Western civilization—a product of scientific and technological progress, of the industrial revolution, of the sweeping economic and social changes brought about by capitalism—and modernity as an aesthetic concept. (41)[12]

Iris Zavala addresses the issue of *modernismo* and the Latin American revolution by discussing an article published by Venezuelan columnist Emilio Coll in the French symbolist journal *Le Mercure de France* in 1897. This journal had inaugurated a new section called "Latin American News" where Coll's article appeared as the first column. The Venezuelan writer identified the literary movement known as *modernismo* with the Cuban struggle for independence: "The first symptoms of the Cuban insurrection have coincided with an intellectual and artistic movement common to all of Latin America" (qtd. in Zavala, "1898" 43). Coll develops his ideas further by explaining that this insurrection has a double meaning: while in the Antilles this is an indicator for national liberation, in other Latin American countries, which had gained their independence decades before, it means a response to the traditions imposed by Spain.[13] Zavala also points out, however, that not all *modernista* writers were like Coll. Many were "marked philistines who just pretended to be avant-garde and rebellious." They were those who "created works without contents, without history and future; empty displays of words, without fundamental tension, not destined for significant transformation" (45–46).[14] Other authors who give insightful information on the subject are Angel Rama, Rafael Gutiérrez Girardot, and César Graña.[15]

Saúl Yurkievich summarizes this literary revolution in quite precise terms:

> To return to the *modernistas* means to safeguard the option of stylization, of sublimation, . . . as antidotes against alienated existence, as compensatory measures to balance the restrictions of empirical reality. . . . It means to preserve the power of subversion, the capacity for imaginative recreation of factual experience. To preserve what is gratuitous, unexpected and surprising—the chimerical dimension. To fulfill desire through esthetic creation and balance it against the reductive violence of the real world. (7–9)[16]

When Octavio Paz defined romanticism in 1974 not only as a literary movement but also as "a new morality, a new eroticism, and a new politics"

(58), he could have been discussing *modernismo* as well. This comparison is especially evident in the importance of the erotic to both movements. As Cathy Jrade argues, "for virtually all the *modernista* writers, erotic passion is the most easily identifiable aspect of nature that has been inhibited or destroyed by the social order" (*Modernismo* 22).

From a Marxist perspective, François Pérus's study on *modernismo* and Rubén Darío, as its best representative, constitutes the first part of a larger project of "historical and sociological interpretation of the most significant literary currents of modern and contemporary Latin America" (9). Pérus identifies the second part of his project as the study of the "social novel," which emerges during the period between 1910–1950, and concludes the third part with the study of what he refers to as the "new narrative" that took place during the 1960's.[17] He also reminds us that "intellectual production does not generate directly from the material base, but rather it always operates over a pre-existing cultural environment, which it perceives itself as autonomous" (20). Pérus also notes as "a fact of the utmost importance" that

> literature cannot be considered as a mechanical and automatic secretion of the social structure, nor as a simple *epifenómeno* of ideology. It simply is a *process of production* socially determined, which operates in a specific manner on a level equally specific, of the system of ideas, images, and social representations, to which literature, however, cannot be reduced. (38)[18]

In sum, the last three decades of the nineteenth century marked the entrance of Spanish America into modernity. It was a moment of great political and economic upheaval, and writers of the time, aware of these changes taking place in all aspects of society, were making conscious efforts to be a part of the making of this new world order. The old colonial models were left behind, and a new language needed to be created to accommodate the new ways of thinking and experiencing life. Far from being involved in the creation of a superficial form of art standing for its own sake, *modernista* writers were most honest and sincere in searching for new avenues by which to show their social and political involvement.

Let us see now how the Uruguayan poet Delmira Agustini fits into this scenario. Since *modernismo* is the first Spanish American movement occupied with matters brought along by modernity, states Jrade, it is also the one movement marking "fundamental shifts in the roles assigned to the poet, language, and literature" (2). From *modernismo*, Agustini utilizes the kind of exotic images that had already been used by the French Parnassians and symbolists: foreign lands, for instance, become points of reference to satisfy that need of lost and desired worlds. As they are in *modernismo*, princesses, fairies, magicians, and muses also become important figures in Agustini's discourse. The Far East, with its enigmas and legends, incenses, pearls and perfume, and classical antiquity, with mythological figures such as Aeolus, Venus, and Helen, also appear in her poetry. The element of color, so important for the symbolists, is at times directly mentioned in Agustini's poetry, (for example, "gray muse," "blue sail," "white camellias") or is indirectly suggested through images which contain it (for example, "honey," "fierce of rubies," or "color of fire"). One can therefore see in Agustini's production the cosmopolitanism mentioned by Monguió as part of the *modernista* esthetics. Starting with the poem "The Statue" (La estatua), Agustini introduces a vocabulary that includes marble figures, monuments of dumb stone, and emperors. It is also in this poem that, for the first time, Agustini introduces the notion of race, which will have a fundamental importance in the poet's work.[19]

At the same time, and as the poet slowly moves away from the *modernista* imagery, a new group of images starts appearing in her discourse. These new images are more subjective and based primarily on an inner dialogue between the poet and her own self, her inner poetic voice. The appearance of this new aesthetic model occurs in the poet's work as early as in her first book of 1907. *The White Book (Fragile)* contains at the end an appendix or subsection that includes only seven poems reunited under the subtitle "Rosy Fringe." The images in these poems are extremely vivid and powerful; they contain visions of death, in which particularly women's sexuality and insatiable desire reign supreme in her poetic discourse. In their erotic essence and overtones, Agustini's images place her close to the ancient Greek lyric poet Sappho, and in their passionate character they remind us of those of the Italian poet Gabriel D'Annunzio (1863–1938). And images of such creatures as black ravens, larvae, worms, and serpents, all used to express Agustini's burning desire, remind us of the surprisingly metaphorical language (reflecting the continued influence of romanticism) in the naturalist novels of Emile Zola (1840–1902).

In the third and last book of Agustini's poems, the swan, an emblem of the inspiration of poets from ancient to modern times, but symbol *par excellence* of *modernismo*, makes its appearance in the poet's discourse. Agustini's swan appears as a phallic figure, a lover of the poet in the clarity of an erotic lake that reflects the poet's thoughts—as she would proclaim in her poem "The Swan" (El cisne). The myth of Zeus and Leda—in which the god disguises himself as a swan in order to seduce Leda, queen of the night—has been recreated by many poets throughout history. In general, the poet acts as a narrator observing and describing the seduction and the love-making occurring in the lake. What is different and important about Agustini's swan is that the poet symbolically assumes the role of Leda herself, thus incorporating her own voice into the poetic discourse. This results in the creation of a highly sensuous and erotic poem.[20]

However, Agustini's poetry also centers around the figure of the male, who appears as the unifying object of both devotion and attention, but who the poet sees as unreachable. This man, who is desired and loved, and who embodies, epitomizes, and represents all men who are desired and loved, makes his appearance in her poetic chamber from very early in her literary production. This man, metaphor of all men, represents in Agustini's discourse the *eternal masculine, the eternal lover,* with whom she shares her own sexuality, which she has chosen to be the center of her aesthetics. In *The Rosary of Eros*, a collection of five poems published posthumously and based upon the mysteries of the Catholic rosary of the Virgin Mary, Agustini reaches the pinnacle in her literary production. In general terms, *The Rosary of Eros* is the most transgressive of all of Agustini's works, for the poet subverts the original intention of the Christian rosary and replaces it with a rosary said in praise and homage to Eros, the Greek god of love.

Throughout her literary career, Agustini experimented with different types of verses and of poems, the sonnet being the most frequently used. Nevertheless, as she matured as a poet and as a human being, Agustini progressively abandoned the sonnet and became freer in the fabric of her work. This spirit of total freedom emanating from her poetry, particularly in her later work, the audacious erotic images she employs, which seem to deviate from those accepted by the society of her time, and the clear effort to make conscious the instinct as well as dark forces of the human being, associate Agustini with the avant-garde movement. At the same time, the exaltation of those original images united with the exquisiteness of her metaphors make Agustini a forerunner of *ultraísmo.*[21]

Delmira Agustini was the forerunner of other female poets at the turn of the century who continued with this kind of feminist debate—namely the struggle to place women as equal to men in many aspects, of which the celebration of sexuality is a fundamental one. As could be expected, her erotic message and sexual discourse were silenced or ignored by the society of her time, and for several decades following Agustini's death, critics systematically attempted to *desexualize* her work. Since Agustini's poetry can be read on different levels, critics of the first five decades of the last century tried to convert her erotic message into something metaphysical or mystical, in order to at least acknowledge her talent and pay tribute to her voice. Alberto Zum Felde was the most influential leader in this conscious effort to desexualize her poetry.[22] Nonetheless, recent Agustini criticism has contributed to a much better understanding of the poet's work, and under the influence of recent literary theories and tendencies, such as feminist studies, gender studies, and women's studies in particular, it is clearer now what she was able to accomplish with her poetry. Nearly one hundred years ago, Delmira Agustini announced a new kind of woman: a woman equal to men in practicing and celebrating sexuality.

In spite of the ignorance and prejudice of traditional Agustini criticism, the first six or seven decades of the 1900s produced a few positive and useful studies of the poet's work. The earliest example of insightful criticism on the poet is "Carta abierta a Delmira Agustini," an open letter written by Uruguayan scholar Alberto Zum Felde in 1914. Ofelia Machado Bonet's extensive biography and critical analysis of Agustini's poetry in 1944 is another important early piece of criticism, in which the Uruguayan writer analyzes Agustini's work objectively for what it is, without any prejudice or attempt to alter the poet's message. Also very important are Emir Rodríguez Monegal's contribution in 1969, *Sexo y poesía en el 900 uruguayo: los extraños destinos de Roberto y Delmira*, book that offers a detailed study of the time and the society in which Delmira Agustini wrote, as well as Alfonsina Storni's positive evaluation of Agustini's work, for the Argentine poet was fighting for the same cause as Agustini, and both poets were immersed in a similar feminist debate (44). Noteworthy, too, is Uruguayan scholar Arturo Sergio Visca, who, in spite of his lack of feminist vision, suggests through his writings on Agustini that he did not join the literary generation of critics who believed she was a mystical or metaphysical poet ("La poesía" 5).

In the last decades of the twentieth century, there was a positive change towards the vision and understanding of human sexuality, particularly that of women, as a result, at least in part, of the positive contribution of the feminist movement. This change has helped to bring about fundamental changes in the fabric of society in general and in literary criticism in particular. Thus, recent approaches to Agustini's poetry have replaced the old mystical-metaphysical ornaments with social realities, in which Delmira Agustini is understood as a provocative and transgressive figure, and as such, now fully acknowledged and accepted. These new critical approaches, not only in Uruguay but also in various other countries, have been giving smoke signals—but with the kind of smoke that cleans rather than asphyxiates—for approximately the last twenty-five years, during which time the language has also dramatically changed and no longer resorts to rhetorical euphemisms.

The New Critical Approach to Agustini's Work

Taking into account that most contributions to this new critical approach to Agustini have been published in Spanish, I review in the following pages the most relevant criticism in order to give both scholars and students interested in research on Agustini easier access to these secondary sources.

Typical of the new critical approach to Agustini's work is Argentinian scholar Silvia Molloy's essay comparing the treatment of the swan in Delmira Agustini and Rubén Darío. The critic analyzes, for instance, Agustini's eroticism, which she describes as something that "needs to be said, to be inscribed, not as the whimper of a woman vanquished, that gets lost in the winds, but as the triumphant, terrible [cry of] pleasure" (66). Molloy identifies the "erotic vampirism" that causes the "yearning ego to be drained of desire" (67). And even more important, her criticism does not hesitate to give the poet an active sexual position, in equal terms with the male:

> The habitual erotic image—the spilling of the male inside the glorified female body—that appears in Darío in connection with Leda . . . is subverted in Agustini: it is the I [ego], the woman, who has fulfilled the white swan . . . giving it substance, and using itself up. (67)[23]

Patricia Varas, in turn, analyzes the poet's work and defines it as "an effort of creation of the human being, as way to free the poetic *I* that includes the liberation of the authorial *I*" (134). Varas maintains that this "calculated effort is a strategy that is not influenced but rather shaped, by the gender of the author, the epoch, and the literary movement of the time: *modernismo*" (134). She also argues that Agustini "has chosen the erotic/sexual frame in order to build her poetic and authorial being," and adds that

> hyper-sensitivity in Agustini is the result of a mental struggle against the barriers imposed by society. Agustini experiences in her own flesh what men historically have defined as "the essence of the feminine," and now she wants to make a definition of femininity through her poetry. (148)

Uruguayan critic and scholar Uruguay Cortazzo, maintains in his criticism of Agustini that "Spanish American *modernismo* made of sexuality one of its aesthetic foundations," and he adds that "Uruguayan *modernismo*," in particular "carried those foundations to an extreme, and made an authentic proposal of a sexual revolution" (195). According to Cortazzo, this revolution was promoted by three representatives of the literary generation of 1900's in Montevideo: First, Julio Herrera y Reissig, who based his poetic aesthetic in the human body proposing a new approach to poetry which presupposes a reader highly trained in his/her own sensual potential; second, Delmira Agustini, who "elaborates a gigantic myth of sexual freedom, which announces the appearance of a new type of woman" (195); and third, Roberto de las Carreras, who "through his literary pamphlets . . . links his sexual esthetics to a revolutionary theory: anarchic-socialism, philosophy closely tied to anarchic-individualism" (195). In Cortazzo's view "Delmira Agustini's poetry questions in a radical manner, the socially valid image of women. . . because by vindicating, in such an exuberant fashion, desire and pleasure," the poet "presents herself as a woman sexually active, and in equal position with the male" (197).

Margaret Bruzelius argues that Agustini "took the version of decadence offered to her by *modernismo,* especially as represented by Rubén Darío, and used it to create extraordinarily intense poetry of explicitly sexual female desire" (52). Bruzelius surmises that "nineteenth-century fascination with the *femme fatale* may have reached its apogee in the figure of the Vampire[,] that marble white silent woman, with luxuriant hair, heavy lidded eyes and blood red lips" (51). This nightmarelike fantasy, the representation of female power incarnated in the vampire, would be directly related to a literary tradition from Edgar Allan Poe to Charles Baudelarie and then to the French and British decadent authors. Bruzelius considers Agustini to be one of the few women who participated in this decadent literary tradition by making herself a vampire femme fatale noting that "the female vampire, unlike many other seductive women, is firmly associated with the ability to speak, to seduce with language, to write." Thus, "Agustini creates a poetic persona as a monstrous female, a revenant who summons the male she desires from the grave" (55). Adopting this poetic persona, Agustini infuses with new life "the worn out images of the symbolists" (59). Agustini's work is saturated with the image of the femme fatale "the dreamer possessed," but with the essential difference that "this fatal woman is not the creation of male desire and fear, but of a female desire that authorizes itself" (59). In her poetry, according to Bruzelius, Agustini "constructs a female voice which gradually frees itself to express female sexual desire" (59).

American critic and scholar Gwen Kirkpatrick explores the literary space in which Agustini is inscribed. For Kirkpatrick, *modernista* poetry of this period coexists with naturalistic prose, both being forerunners of the avant-garde. Referring to Agustini as well as Herrera y Reissig, Kirkpatrick notes that the differences and interruptions of the traditional *modernista* discourse indicate that both Agustini and Herrera y Reissig "reject the weight of tradition through their somewhat anarchic individualism" ("Limits 311). Kirkpatrick identifies "the sonnet" as the favorite poetic form for both writers: "Its rigor, enclosure, and poetic closure issue to them an invitation to shake its structure from within by exaggeration, fragmentation, or elliptical breaks in meaning"

(311). In Agustini's poetry, this exaggeration of the limits established by tradition is even more obvious, accentuating her refusal "to mediate between individualistic conscience and an external world" (311). Kirkpatrick also analyzes Georges Bataille's work, especially his concept of eroticism, the fascination that eroticism has with death, and its continuous dynamics of dislocation and dissolution. For Kirkpatrick, the play of eroticism in the works of both Agustini and Herrera y Reissig "can make clearer their articulation between two poetic epochs, and between the poetry and the prose of their times" (312). On the surface of their poetry lie "images and exchanges usually reserved for the prose of the period," and in the interruptions and vagueness suggested by ellipsis, "they suggest the more radical experiments of the poets who will follow" (312).

Asunción Horno-Delgado studies the frequency with which Agustini incorporates "the eyes" in her work, referring particularly to what she calls Agustini's "own lyric voice." (101). The critic also notices that, the statue "is the symbol par excellence in Agustini's poetry, in which the woman suffers from a `fear of immobility,' as expressed, for example by Alfonsina Storni" (106). Analyzing the poem "Plegaria" (Entreaty), Horno-Delgado speculates on the meaning of one of the verses—"Mirar tan lejos" (Looking far away)— and suggests that this image "could refer to the repressive situation in which women lived at that time, always putting pleasure aside, for the sake of defending, unwillingly, patriarchal systems which paralyzed them" (106). Horno-Delgado concludes that "Agustini—being conscious of such a problem—placed her writing in the service of her own liberation, thus demonstrating that both sexual activity and the initiative of desire, are not exclusive to the male" (106). "Delmira Agustini," Horno-Delgado adds, "lived her own body with the greatest intensity, thus being capable of perceiving widely what affected or enchanted the psychology of others" (106).

Using a complex but not always convincing Freudian approach, Gisela Norat explores the topics of vampirism, sadism, and masochism in Agustini's work. Her hypothesis is that Agustini's central inner conflict has its origin in the psychotic relation the poet had with her mother, a perception undoubtedly influenced by reading Emir Rodríguez Monegal's early criticism. Norat's analysis of the texts, which indeed throw light upon a sadomasochistic tendencies and vampirelike postures, is sophisticated, and the examples she uses are as clear as they are precise. The critic points out that, based on the supposedly sadomasochistic relationship the poet had with the male, the ulterior motive, from the point of view of the unconscious, is the repressed aggression against María Murtfeldt, her mother. However, even if there had been an overprotective relationship between Agustini and her parents, it does not necessarily mean that this relationship was destructive. Instead, just the opposite could be the case, namely: a beneficial influence, a positive impact, which protected the poet against her social environment and allowed her to explore her creative potential.[24] For Norat, Agustini's position "leads her to elaborate a poetic Eros that functions as a wall of resistance against the repression she experiences in a patriarchal society," using eroticism as "the instrument that the poet chooses for transgression" (153). Nevertheless, this fairly convincing affirmation, and evaluation of the work, is scrutinized under the light of Electra's complex and of the penis envy women feel toward men during their psychological development and through the diverse stages the female unconscious goes through during its development. Norat's conclusion is that

> Delmira Agustini is the vampire that takes revenge against her mother for having sucked the daughter's blood, thus paralyzing her freedom under the mother's vigilant eye, and the excessively possessive love of the mother saps, in a symbolic manner, the daughter's life. (156)

The subject of beheading in the poet's work, which is of extreme importance to modern scholars, also acquires with Norat a different significance. It is no longer the conquering of the male by means of obtaining his head—following the Salomé tradition—but rather his beheading is a Freudian symbol of castration. If the "true reason behind the manifestations of violence— abundant in Agustini's poetry—lies in an unconscious conflict with her mother," then by "punishing the male, Agustini, in reality, is defending herself against the mother" as well. (160).

American scholar Doris Stephens makes a unique and valuable contribution to Agustini criticism by closely analyzing the poet's work and meticulously dissecting and identifying each one of the elements that constitute, according to Stephens, a carefully planned poetic theory with elements such as light, color, strength, beauty, and the idea of the muse. Stephens makes the point that Agustini's "desire for musicality in her poetry" may have been encouraged "by the *modernistas* and Verlaine, and also by the poet's own knowledge of music" (80).[25] Mario Alvarez analyzes Agustini's work from a feminist literary critical perspective. For him,

> women have always been, of course, in the center of erotic poetry, but that approach had mostly been addressed, with some few exceptions, from the male's point of view, particularly from the point of view of a male certain of his superiority. In that model, women appeared as the object of eroticism, whether purely sexual or integrated into personal and complex feelings. Delmira's novelty and contribution was just to present a woman, herself, as an erotic object. Needless to say, the poet's audacious attitude also reflected what other women were questioning at the time: the recognition of women's political and civil rights, her dignified role in society, and so on. (38)

What is interesting here is that after having speculated something so coherent and possible—which to a certain extent supports Cortazzo's theory on the subject of sexual-political revolution—Alvarez seemingly contradicts his argument, when he makes the surprising confession:

> We could be committing an error, however, if we believed that Delmira's sexual and erotic poetry is founded and revolves around the challenge to an old and harsh social order imposed on women, or that her poetry reflects an overthrowing of that order and norms on the part of the poet's conscience. (38–39)

Of great interest is John Burt's reading of Agustini based on new renderings of some episodes of classical mythology. In using mythological episodes, Agustini does not, according to Burt's essay "The Personalization of Classical Myth in Delmira Agustini," assume the traditional role of the narrator, but rather becomes one of the *dramatis personae* during the enactment of the mythological plot. Burt suggests, and sustains his thesis with clear and precise examples, that behind the poem "The Wings," one can find the myth of Icarus incarnated in Delmira; that in "The Swan" Delmira plays the role of Leda (we should be reminded here of Silvia Molloy's reading of "The Swan," wherein the poet assumes the role of Leda, the queen of the night, to be penetrated by the swan's beak); and that in the poem "Another Lineage," one can find the myth of Cupid and Psyche, Cupid being to Roman mythology what Eros is to Greek mythology. The poem "Your Mouth" would incorporate the myth of Pygmalion, and finally, "The Ineffable" would suggest the myth of Prometheus. Burt concludes that Delmira,

> in the clouded atmosphere of the Gods, offers herself freely on the altar of love with the thought that her lover and she were almost of divine nature. Unfortunately, no human male could share that clouded foggy atmosphere with her, thus forcing her in the end, to confront that other world alone, which renders her act of self-sacrifice so tragic. (123)

Margarita Rojas and Flora Ovares re-examine the relationship between the feminine and the literary by focusing on the topic of eroticism, the transgressive treatment of the religious environment, and the archetypal images of shadow and light. Their analysis of the sonnet "The Intruder" (El intruso) and the poem "Vision" (Visión), both approached from the critical perspective of French structuralism (Barthes, Todorov), concentrates on the observation of the amorous subjects, the double, the hermaphroditic figure, the swan and the serpent, and necrophilia as some ingredients of the sexual themes.

For Spanish scholar Tina Fernández Escaja, the complexity of Agustini's esthetics gravitates around a discourse of desire, the desire to have access to the word, its metapoetic effect, and unity both in a sexual and nominal manner, for example, tongue and rose, sex and poem. Fernández Escaja approaches Agustini's work from a feminist perspective, which allows her to analyze the situation of women at the turn of the century, particularly in Uruguay. She divides Agustini's production into two distinct periods, which she associates with two myths: the myth of Ofelia, Ofelia lying upon the river of conscience, in an apparently passive and receptive attitude, associating this myth with Agustini's early production, *The White Book (Fragile)* (1907); and the myth of Orpheus, most notably in *The Empty Chalices* (1913). Both poetic spheres—of Ofelias's reception and Orpheus's dismemberment—are integrated into the image of God's head lying in the hands of the poet, in order to incorporate the modern metaphor of desire for both sexual and linguistic unity. Fernández Escaja concludes that the conflict between essential dualities defines the poet's life and work: Logos and Eros, spirit and flesh, what is human and what is divine. This conflict is neutralized in an intermediate place: the space of desire. This desire for legitimation of both personal and artistic being distinguishes the aesthetics of Agustini's poetry: the eagerness of reaching with the tongue, with the word, the heart of the rose.[26]

In her essay "[D]élmira: La representación del hombre en la poesía de Agustini," Uruguayan critic and scholar Estela Valverde departs from the interpretations of Agustini as "the girl," "the vampire," "the masochist," or "the sadist." Noting that Agustini's work has been accepted in terms of a split of her personality between the innocent virgin, carefully constructed for her mother, and the voluptuous whore, projected in her poetry, Valverde is nevertheless unconvinced by this traditional approach and examines the manner in which the poet creates the figure of the male who inspires and finally destroys her.[27]

María Elena Barreiro-Armstrong also uses these dialectics of identities and dualities and interprets Agustini's work as the empty existence for the lyric *I (ego)* of the woman, her search of the male *you*, the desire of reaching unity with that *you*, and the emptiness to which the lyric *I* returns after having lost that *you*. To Barreiro-Armstrong, the center of that dramatic tension between the *you* and the *I* is Eros himself: He is both threshold and cause and effect of *unity*, and therefore Eros is the central metaphor of Agustini's work, the production that the poet conceives in a pendular fashion.

American scholar Linda Key Davis East argues that Delmira Agustini's poetry "has lasting value precisely because it expresses how all Latin America feels by means of her own mental—not physical—experience" (10). She adds that Agustini's "place in literary history and proper criticism of her poetry rest on the appreciation of this fundamental point" (10). For Davis East, Agustini's images contain archetypal symbols, and the critic identifies "light" not only as an image but also as a concept. Contrary to traditional criticism on Agustini, which "has centered its observations on the body and the apparently erotic elements of her poetry—relating them to the poet's life," Davis East centers her own study primarily "on the mental processes that these elements symbolized" (26). Davis East argues that Agustini's poetry suggests an obsession with the mind and knowledge. Although she does not advocate the theory of the double personality, Davis East does believe that "the poet can only express herself when she has managed to disassociate herself from the exterior world" (65). To Agustini "the poetic act is a path of conscience that leads to knowledge" (74). Davis East identifies Agustini's *lyric I*, the relation to the *you*, and the search of her own identity, as major points in the poet's discourse. She also comments on the personification of Leda in "The Swan."

Roberto Lima analyzes the meaning of libido as sexual appetite and the way in which society has traditionally respected, or not respected, its expressions. "If the male has to abide by moral norms which are restrictive of his sexual instinct, he has always found the way to subvert and free himself from those norms and the bonds of marriage, in order to satisfy the urges of his libido" (42). In contrast, "the expression of a woman's sexual appetite outside marriage has been forbidden by a hypocritical attitude, which tolerates the evasion of the single or married male, but which condemns as adulterous that of a married woman and as prostitution that of a single one" and labels a woman, but not a man, dishonest (42-43). Lima contends that "this unjust lack of balance has fostered the development of a subversive trend among those individuals who need to give a vital expression to their libido" and singles out the contemporary feminist movement, which "has as one of its goals the sexual freedom of women" (43). It is in this context that Lima analyzes Agustini's work, identifying Delmira's libido as it appears in representative poems and themes. The idea of a "vaginal delirium"—the critic says— is what best characterizes Delmira Agustini's attitude regarding her own libido. "Fierce of Love" offers Lima the opportunity to see that delirium manifested in a bestial context, from which emerges a male statue that, according to Lima, does not inspire in the poet esthetic or historical admiration, but rather a desire for the "phallic object she has to possess" (45).

"The decisive shift that actually signals an essential reorientation away from the *modernista* agenda," notes Cathy Jrade, "comes when the overall optimism of *modernismo* gives way to a more pervasive doubt and the abiding faith in a divine order is eroded by penetrating anguish" (*Modernismo* 94). According to Jrade, this creates a "corrosive skepticism," and, moreover, the search for beauty and logic becomes secondary, as "art focuses on and aggressively confronts what is interpreted to be an increasingly hostile environment" (94). In Jrade's view, this fundamental change is what defines *la vanguardia*, the avant-garde. Like Gwen Kirkpatrick, Jrade considers Delmira Agustini, as well as Leopoldo Lugones and Julio Herrera y Reissig, as writers who "drew upon the *modernista* impetus toward change and pushed further the expansion of the poetic repertoire in Spanish" (94). She argues that these poets anticipated "the movement's transformation," thus making them forerunners of the Hispanic avant-garde; "whether she intended to or not, Delmira Agustini . . . explores the limits of the *modernista* conceptions of existence and poetry" (133).

Finally, Diane E. Marting, in her discussion of female sexuality as a dangerous topic linked to themes of social justice for women, agrees with Angel Rama, who notes:

> That is what happened with Delmira Agustini: women's arts are beginning to exist in Uruguay due to her. She died when two disparate functions, both imposed by the new society of the 1900s, entered into conflict inside her: the mystification of the conventional bourgeois woman and her independence as a being of amorous sensuality.[28] (Prologue 4)

"Murdered by her ex-husband, the poet Agustini represents"—according to Marting—"an extreme case of victimization by Montevideo high society's particular juncture of patriarchal values":

> The ferociousness of the attack against Agustini was not typical, but her brave writing and tragic death illustrate in broad outline some of the difficult choices and negative consequences for women authors and artists who before the 1960s flaunted strictures regarding the woman writer and female sexuality. (4)

Like other great women artists of the twentieth century, for example the Mexican artist Frida Kahlo, the American poet Sylvia Plath, and the American dancer Isadora Duncan, Delmira Agustini has come to be seen as representative of the difficult and conflicting roles a woman must play when she finds herself ahead of the society into which she was born. Some may disguise their true identities under male pen names; others may need to soften their message to avoid appearing too outrageous to their audiences; others may compromise in order to be gradually accepted; but, in fact, many creative women become victims, because society is often not prepared to accept them.

NOTES

1. All three books were published in Montevideo by Orsini M. Bertani, an Italian intellectual, a naturalized Uruguayan, and a former member of the anarchist party.

Expatriated from Italy, Bertani went first to Argentina and afterwards to Uruguay, where he arrived during the first years of the century along with other members of the anarchist party. A member of the Montevidean literary intellectual community, he belonged to the group of writers and political activists who gathered at the famous Polo Bamba coffee house—the most prestigious intellectual center of that moment. Between the beginning of the century and 1913, Bertani contributed a great deal to the cultural development of the city by opening a small publishing house in the back room of his own bookstore, where he published a large number of volumes of both prose and poetry written by national and international writers of the time.

2. For an in-depth study of this period of their lives, see Ofelia Machado Bonet; also, Clara Silva, *Genio y figura de Delmira Agustini*; Alejandro Cáceres, "Doña María Murtfeld Triaca de Agustini."

3. According to Clara Silva, Agustini was quoted by her mother; see *Genio y figura*. It is important to note that the "vulgarity" she refers to may not mean that she considered Enrique Job to be a vulgar (rough, bad-mannered) man but rather that she considered married life and domesticity to be vulgar.

4. The union of church and state appears legitimated in the 1830 constitution, where it is said that the official religion of the state is the Roman Catholic Apostolic. The separation of church and state occurred with the second constitution of March 1, 1919. President Batlle ordered the removal of all Catholic religious symbols in 1906. His administration fostered indeed the separations process. See Caetano; and Caetano and Geymonat.

5. Like other critics writing on this subject, I will employ throughout this work the Spanish noun *modernismo* and the adjectives *modernista* and *modernistas* (to distinguish them from the English linguistically but not contextually equivalent "modernism" and "modernist") to refer to the literary movement that flourished in Spanish America between 1870 and 1920 approximately. For a detailed study on the subject, see Cathy Jrade, *Modernismo, Modernity, and the Development of Spanish American Literature*.

6. The adjective *cachondo* in vulgar Spanish means sexually aroused, but I consider "flirting" to be the closest possible translation, although "to flirt" does not necessarily imply a sexual move. On the other hand, the noun *pudor* does not necessarily translate as "candor" but rather as "modesty" or "decorum." *Candor* in English means "frankness" or "sincerity" of expression. Of all these possibilities, I believe that *Modesty and Flirting* is still the closest choice. It has been suggested that an alternative translation could also be *Modesty and the Sex Drive*. In sum, the idea behind the two nouns represents the game between the male and the female—his chasing her, her escaping from him, as a prelude to the sexual encounter. See also Claudia Giaudrone and Nilo Berriel, *El pudor, la cachondez, de Julio Herrera y Reissig*.

7. The Charrúa Indians were one of the tribes living in what is today the territory of Uruguay when the Spaniards arrived. They were extremely brave, and because of that they could not be integrated into civilized society. In the early part of the twentieth century they were finally exterminated. The "new Charrúas" in Herrera y Reissig's expression implies a sarcastic way to label the Uruguayan population at the time.

8. This group of poems constitutes perhaps the most difficult, hermetic, and intricate sample of Agustini's writings. The posthumous poems are neither well known nor easy to understand. Indeed, they are highly complex, and, in my interpretation, involve the notions of Jungian collective unconscious and theory of archetypes, as well as medieval alchemy and the organization, meaning, and proper recitation of the Christian rosary of the Virgin Mary. See my introduction to *Delmira Agustini: Poesías completas*, pp. 62–69.

9. He refers to Spanish critic and novelist Juan Valera (1824–1905), forerunner on the criticism of Darío's work, who already uses the adjective *cosmopolita* when evaluating, in 1888, Darío's *Azul*. Monguió refers also to José Enrique Rodó (1872–1917), who believed that "the poets who may want to express in a manner universally intelligible for the superior souls, educated and humane ways of thinking and feeling, should renounce to a true stamp of original Americanism, meaning that they must be culturally and expressively cosmopolitan" (78). He also refers to Argentine critic and writer Anderson Imbert, who in 1961 also employs the same adjective when discussing Darío's work. Moreover, he points out that between 1888 and 1961 many other critics have also used the same idea when discussing works written not only by Rubén Darío, but by other *modernista* authors. And the critic adds that Darío himself employed this term when referring to the *modernista* revolution in Hispanic letters.

10. Men like Rodó, with his *Ariel* (1900), Darío with his *Cantos de vida y esperanza* (1905), and Lugones with his *Odas seculares* (1910) attempted to emphasize Spanish Americanism. "These *modernista* authors, so cosmopolitan in their love for the ideal, knew how to turn their eyes to *América* . . . to exult the beautiful values they believed were essential to the integrity of their tradition and their land" (Rodó qtd. in Monguió 86).

11. While the philosophical origins of modernity can be traced to the Renaissance, notes Jrade, the characteristics of modernity or modern times become more clear within the second half of the eighteenth century and are related to scientific and technological knowledge, the Industrial Revolution, and the changes brought about by capitalism. The critic explores "the nature of the connection between *modernismo* and modernity, thereby modifying the way in which the movement is perceived"

(*Modernismo* 2). Jrade also maintains that all the social and political changes that occurred as a consequence of modern life encouraged literary responses very different from those of previous movements. Furthermore, Jrade states that since *modernismo* is the first Spanish American movement occupied with matters associated with the onset of modernity, it is also the one movement marking "fundamental shifts in the roles assigned to the poet, language, and literature" (2). She concludes by affirming that all these changes have continued influencing recent developments in Spanish American literature, placing it "in the much contested rubric of postmodernity" (2).

12. Calinescu calls the first modernity the "bourgeois idea of modernity," which has continued with the traditions of former periods "in the history of the modern idea" (41). These traditions—states the critic—are the "doctrine of progress, the confidence in the beneficial possibilities of science and technology, the concern with time . . . like any other commodity" that has a value in monetary terms, "the cult of reason, and the ideal of freedom . . . the orientation towards pragmatism, and the cult of action and success" (41). All these values were promoted in "the triumphant civilization established by the middle class" (42). On the contrary, the other modernity, which he calls "cultural modernity" (42) was from its romantic beginnings inclined towards radical antibourgeois attitudes. This modernity, says Calinescu, reflected a disgust with the middle class scale of values, a discomfort which was expressed in a variety of ways including, rebellion, anarchy, and aristocratic self-exile. To Calinescu, "the history of the alienation of the modern writer starts with the romantic movement," and in an earlier stage, "the object of hatred and ridicule is *philistinism*, a typical form of middle class hypocrisy" (43).

13. According to Coll, *modernismo* meant for the Latin American writers a revolution in "Art." Zavala discusses the idea that Art cannot be divorced from history nor creative activities from politics, "for in the radical perspective of the arts, they are a solid matrimony. And it is in precisely this way that the Latin American *modernistas* viewed their own struggle at the turn of the century" ("1898" 43). This Marxist perspective implies "studying art as conditioned by time, and by the needs and hopes of particular historical situations" (44). *Modernista* writers were, of course, "lovers of beauty," explains Zavala, but "to them Art was also an activity of self-knowledge, self-determination, cultural and national independence" (44). *Modernismo*

> did not mean a revolution in aesthetic practices alone; they were integrating in a very particular artistic language the experiences of new countries, and they hoped to do it in a revolutionary language which would enable them to express their own particular conceptions of the world. By destroying old forms, they left as a legacy to generations of Latin Americans a method of constructive

fantasy, which would be later linked with the theme of revolution and class struggle: César Vallejo and Pablo Neruda offered a way of social decisions with clear conscience. (44–45)

14. When discussing the works of Enrique González Martínez and his memorable sonnet "Tuércele el cuello al cisne . . ." (Twist the neck of the swan . . .), which for many had traditionally meant the end of *modernismo,* and the beginning of what for some was *postmodernismo,* Cathy Jrade emphasizes the error those early critics had made:

> Contrary to their contention, the "swans of deceitful plumage" (cisnes de engañoso plumaje) to which González Martínez refers, did not belong to *modernista* poets, but rather, as he himself would make clear, to the myriad, now long-forgotten, hack imitators who echoed the language of *modernismo,* its opulence, elegance, and ornamentation, without comprehending the underlying issue that defined *modernista* poetics. (*Modernismo* 95)

This is the same group that Zavala mentions in her article on Coll's ideas.

15. To Angel Rama, "[t]he onset of modernization around 1870 was the second test facing the lettered city in the nineteenth century" (*The Lettered City* 50), the first test being the independence period. It was "towards the end of the nineteenth century," Rama explains, that in Latin America, "a dissidence began to manifest itself within the lettered city and to configure a body of critical thought" (55). Rama also quotes Uruguayan writer and philosopher Carlos Vaz Ferreira, who once remarked that "those who lived too late to be positivists became Marxists instead—highlighting the way that Latin American intellectuals have selectively adapted successive European doctrines to their own vigorous, internal traditions" (56). Rama moves on to discuss the fact that "Latin American writers lived and wrote in cities and, if possible, capital cities, remaining resolutely urban people, however much they sprinkled their works with the naturalistic details required by the literary vogue of local color" (61). Rama considers José Martí and Rubén Darío as the "two greatest Latin American poets of the period of modernization" (61).

Meanwhile, in discussing the bohemian lifestyle and the utopias, Rafael Gutiérrez Girardot quotes César Graña, who understands the rise of the bohemian lifestyle to be the result of the disappearance of the traditional sponsors who for centuries had supported writers, artists, and musicians. He also refers to

> the establishment of the bourgeois middle class as a dominant class both politically and ideologically; also the rising of technology and industrialization, the democratization of literary life in the cities, the unemployment of intellectuals, besides the *ennui,* the theory of the personal genius, and the

tension between writers, society, and the State. (Graña qtd. in Gutiérrez Girardot, *Modernismo* 176)

16. "Volver a los modernistas significa salvaguardar el recurso a la estilización, a la sublimación, a la libidinación como antídotos contra la existencia alienada, como compensadoras de las restricciones de lo real empírico. Significa alcanzar por el extrañamiento la trascendencia irrealizable en la práctica social, vislumbrar por la utopía la completud que el orden imperante imposibilita. Significa preservar el poder de subversión, la capacidad de recrear imaginativamente la experiencia fáctica. Preservar la gratuidad, lo sorpresivo y sorprendente, la proyección quimérica. Realizar el deseo en la dimensión estética para oponerlo a la represión, a la violencia reductora del mundo factible" (*Celebración* 9).

17. Pérus considers that the selection of these three moments is not theoretically arbitrary, but rather that these periods constitute true milestones around which the global process of modern and contemporary Spanish American literature acquires meaning. Moreover, explains Pérus,

> those "trends" correspond to well defined and highly representative
> moments of the historical development of the continent: implantation of
> the capitalistic way of production of a Latin America inserted in the capitalist-
> imperialist new world order, in the case of *modernismo;* a crisis of the local
> "oligarchic" sector of capitalist development, with an uprising of the lower
> social groups and the middle stages of the political scene, in the case of the
> "social novel" of the period 1910–1950; and a crucial change of direction of
> Latin American groups towards a process of industrialization, and accentuated
> urbanization, with characteristics each time more complex and conflictive of
> articulation with imperialism, in the case of the 'new narrative' of the 60's.
> (9–10)

18. In her article "1898, Modernismo, and the Latin American Revolution," Iris Zavala briefly states one of the fundamental concepts of Marxist criticism regarding art:

> Those who think that Marxist critics are *only* concerned with realist literary
> works that depict revolutionary socialist trends, have missed the point, for the
> study of artistic expression goes well beyond social realism. Marxist analysis,
> to my understanding, implies studying art as conditioned by time, and by the
> needs and hopes of particular historical situations. (44)

19. This notion of "race" can also be found in the philosophies of Friedrich Nietzsche and Arthur Schopenhauer.

20. For more analysis of the swan imagery in Agustini's work, see Molloy.

21. These two aesthetic movements—as well as all other "isms" of the turn of the century—emerged towards the end of the second decade of the twentieth century; by then Delmira Agustini had been dead for about five years. *Ultraísmo*—the Spanish version of the French *dadaism*—appeared in Spain in 1919 by means of the *"Ultra"* *manifesto* signed by a group of young poets, among whom were Guillermo de Torre, Juan Larrea, Gerardo Diego, and Jorge Luis Borges. Once Agustini abandoned the *modernista* imagery, her poetic voice started focusing on the same revolution of the *avant-garde* aesthetics that the group of young *ultraísta* poets was also looking for: A kind of aesthetic revolution that could take the poem to a different level, a different and superior dimension. Cathy Jrade notes that

> [t]he decisive shift that actually signals an essential reorientation away from the *modernista* agenda comes when the overall optimism of *modernismo* gives way to a more pervasive doubt and the abiding faith in a divine order is eroded by penetrating anguish. Confidence that cultural patterns are capable of revealing, evoking, or reflecting transcendental truths is undermined by a corrosive skepticism. The pursuit of formal beauty and logic recedes as art focuses on and aggressively confronts what is interpreted to be an increasingly hostile environment. This profound alteration is what defines *la vanguardia*, the *avant-garde*. (*Modernismo* 94)

She also considers Agustini as a representative of the avant-garde.

22. This was a conscious effort Zum Felde made after the poet died and was probably due to his trying to put distance between himself and the tragedy. It was a matter of politics—they had been quite close, and now he was becoming very famous as a critic and scholar. Nevertheless, in 1914, Zum Felde published an extraordinary open letter to the public that analyzed the poet's work, and it can be considered the earliest example of true and positive criticism on Agustini. See Zum Felde, *Proceso intelectual del Uruguay* and "Carta"; and Cortazzo, "Una hermenéutica machista."

23. See Molloy; this article was also reprinted in *Delmira Agustini: Nuevas penetraciones críticas* (1996): 92–106.

24. This subject was, precisely, the one that suggested to me to undertake a difficult study of the famous letter Enrique Job sent to Delmira once they were separated; indeed, one of my conclusions was the evaluation of how positive the relationship between the parents and the daughter was. See my essay "Doña María Murtfeldt Triaca de Agustini."

25. I find this comment especially convincing, because it coincides with my own criticism and analysis of the fabric of Agustini's poetry. See my introduction to *Delmira Agustini: Poesías completas* , especially pp. 41–44.

26. See also Escaja, "Inventing Borders," "(Auto) Creación," "Autoras modernistas," "On Angels and Androids," and *Salomé decapitada*.

27. It is important to notice that in the poet's name, Delmira, the square brackets around the letter *D* as well as the accent mark on the letter *e* appear this way in the original title of the article. In her narrative, Valverde fuses the woman Delmira and the man she is constructing poetically, in a single being who, in this case, "sees" the person that is creating him.

28. "Así pasó con Delmira Agustini por quien comienza a existir un arte femenino en el Uruguay, y que muere cuando entran en pugna dentro de ella las dos funciones dispares que la nueva sociedad novecientista le impone: la mistificación de la burguesa convencional y su independencia como ente de la sensualidad amorosa" (Marting 4).

BIBLIOGRAPHY

Agustini, Delmira. *Los cálices vacíos*. Ed. O. M. Bertani. Montevideo: El Arte, 1913.

———. *Cantos de la mañana*. Ed. O. M. Bertani. Montevideo: El Arte, 1910.

———. *El libro blanco (Frágil)*. Ed. O. M. Bertani. Montevideo: El Arte, 1907.

———. *Obras completas*. 2 vols. Ed. Maximino García. Montevideo: El Siglo Ilustrado, 1924.

———. *Delmira Agustini: Poesías completas*. Ed. Alejandro Cáceres. Montevideo: Ediciones de la Plaza, 1999.

———. *Poesías completas de Delmira Agustini*. Ed. Alberto Zum Felde. Buenos Aires: Losada, 1944.

Alvar, Manuel. *La poesía de Delmira Agustini*. Sevilla: Escuela de Estudios Hispanoamericanos de Sevilla, 1958.

Alvarez, Mario. *Delmira Agustini*. Montevideo: Arca, 1979.

Anderson Imbert, Enrique. *Historia de la literatura hispanoamericana*. Mexico City: Fondo de cultura económica, 1961.

Barrán, José P., and Benjamín Nahum. *Historia de la sensibilidad en el Uruguay: El disciplinamiento (1860–1920)*. Vol. 2. Montevideo: Banda Oriental, 1990.

———. *El Uruguay del novecientos*. 2nd ed. 3 vols. Montevideo: Banda Oriental, 1990.

Barreiro-Armstrong, María Elena. "Puente de luz: Eros, eje de la estructura pendular en *Los cálices vacíos* de Delmira Agustini." Ph.D. Diss. Middlebury College, 1996.

Bataille, Georges. *Death and Sensuality: A Study of Eroticism and the Taboo*. Trans. Mary Dalwood. New York: Walker, 1962.

———. *La littérature et le mal*. Paris: Gallimard, 1957.

————. *Oeuvres completes.* Vol. 8. Paris: Gallimard, 1976.

————. *La practique de la joie devant la mort.* Paris: Mercure de France, 1967.

Beaupied, Aída. "Otra lectura de `El cisne' de Delmira Agustini." *Letras femeninas* 22 (1996): 131–42.

Berenguer, Amanda. "La paradoja de lo literario en Delmira Agustini." *Delmira Agustini.* Ed. Amanda Berenguer, Arturo Sergio Visca, and José Pedro Díaz. Cuadernos de Literatura, no. 1. Montevideo: Fundación de Cultura Universitaria, 1968. 17–25.

Bruzelius, Margaret. "En el profundo espejo del deseo: Delmira Agustini, Rachilde, and the Vampire." *Revista hispánica moderna* 46 (1993): 51–64.

Burt, John R. "Agustini's Muse." *Chasqui* 17.1 (1988): 61–65.

————. "The Personalization of Classical Myth in Delmira Agustini." *Crítica hispánica* 9.1–2 (1987): 115–24.

Cabrera, Sarandy. "Las poetisas del 900." *Número* 2.6–8 (1950): 162–86.

Cáceres, Alejandro. "Delmira Agustini: An Early Feminist Voice." Lecture given at the Library of Congress, Washington, D.C. Nov. 1997.

————. "Delmira Agustini: La búsqueda de libertad sexual y la construcción del yo." *Delmira Agustini y el Modernismo: Nuevas propuestas de género.* Comp. Tina Escaja. Rosario, Argentina: Beatriz Viterbo Editora, 2000. 257–68.

————, ed. *Delmira Agustini: Poesías completas.* Montevideo: Ediciones de la Paza, 1999.

————. "Delmira Agustini's `Lo inefable': A New Version to Consider for the Study of Variants." July 1996 (unpublished article).

————. "Delmira Agustini: The Search for Sexual Identity and the Construction of Her Self." Paper presented at the Third Annual Hispanic Forum: Delmira Agustini and Modernisms. University of Vermont–Burlington, Sept. 1996.

————. "Delmira Agustini y el silencio de Eros." Lecture given at the National Library of Uruguay. July 1994.

————. "Doña María Murtfeldt Triaca de Agustini: Hipótesis de un secreto." *Delmira Agustini: Nuevas penetraciones críticas.* Ed. Uruguay Cortazzo. Montevideo: Vintén Editor, 1996. 13–47.

Cáceres, Esther de. Prólogo. *Delmira Agustini: Antología.* Vol. 69 of *Colección de Clásicos Uruguayos.* Montevideo: Barreiro, 1965. vii–xlv.

Caetano, Gerado. "Batlle y Ordóñez, José." *Encyclopedia of Latin American History and Culture.* Vol. 1. New York: Scribner's, 1996. 310–311.

Caetano, Gerardo, and Roger Geymonat. *La secularización uruguaya (1859–1919).* Montevideo: Taurus, 1997.

Calinescu, Matei. *Five Faces of Modernity: Modernism, Avant-Garde, Decadence, Kitsch, Postmodernism*. Durnham: Duke UP, 1987.

Calinescu, Matei, and Douwe Fokkema. *Exploring Postmodernism*. Amsterdam: John Benjamins, 1987.

Cortazzo, Uruguay. "Delmira Agustini: Hacia una visión sexo política." *Delmira Agustini y el Modernismo: Nuevas propuestas de género*. Comp. Tina Escaja. Rosario, Argentina: Beatriz Viterbo Editora, 2000. 195–204.

———, ed. *Delmira Agustini: Nuevas penetraciones críticas*. Montevideo: Vintén Editor, 1996.

———. "Una hermenéutica machista: Delmira Agustini en la crítica de Alberto Zum Felde." *Delmira Agustini: Nuevas penetraciones críticas*. Ed. Uruguay Cortazzo. Montevideo: Vintén, 1996. 48–74.

De las Carreras, Roberto. *Salmo a Venus Cavalieri y otras prosas*. Montevideo: Arca, 1967.

Díaz, José Pedro. "Sobre la experiencia poética de Delmira Agustini." *Delmira Agustini*. Ed. Amanda Berenguer, Arturo Sergio Visca, and José Pedro Díaz. Cuadernos de Literatura, no. 1. Montevideo: Fundación de Cultura Universitaria, 1968. 26–36.

Duncan, Isadora. *My Life*. New York: Garden City, 1927.

Ellis, Albert. *The Encyclopedia of Sexual Behavior*. 2 vols. New York: Hawthorn Books, 1961.

East, Linda Key Davis. "The Imaginary Voyage: Evolution of the Poetry of Delmira Agustini." Ph.D. Diss. Stanford, 1981.

Escaja, Tina. "(Auto) Creación y revisionismo en *Los cálices vacíos* de Delmira Agustini." *Bulletin of Hispanic Studies* 75 (1998): 213–28.

———. "Autoras modernistas y la (re)inscripción del cuerpo nacional." *Sexualidad y nación*, ed. Daniel Balderson. Pittsburgh: Instituto Internacional de Literatura Iberoamericana, 2000. 61–75.

———. "Inventing Borders: Women Poets of Modernismo." *Boletín: Fondo de cultura económica—USA* 2 (1994): 2, 3–7.

———. "On Angels and Androids: Spanish American Women Poets Facing Centuries' End." *Hispanófila* 130 (2000): 91–15.

———. *Salomé decapitada: Delmira Agustini y la literatura finisecular de la fragmentación*. New York: Rodopi, 2002.

Fernández Escaja, Tina. "La lengua en la rosa: Dialéctica del deseo en la obra de Delmira Agustini." Ph.D. Diss. University of Pennsylvania, 1993.

Freud, Sigmund. *On the History of the Psycho-Analytic Movement*. Trans. Joan Riviere. New York: Norton, 1966.

García-Pinto, Magdalena. "Eros in Reflection: The Poetry of Delmira Agustini." *Review: Latin American Literature* 48 (1994): 85–89.

Gay, Volney P. *Reading Jung: Science, Psychology and Religion.* Chico, California: Scholars Press, 1984.

Giaudrone, Claudia, and Nilo Berriel, eds. *El pudor, la cachondez.* By Julio Herrera y Reissig. Montevideo: Arca, 1992.

Giot de Badet, André. "Delmira Agustini." *Revue Mondiale* 202.1 (1931): 256–64.

Graña, César. *Modernity and Its Discontents.* New York: Harper Torchbooks, 1967.

Gutiérrez Girardot, Rafael. *Modernismo.* Barcelona: Montesinos, 1983.

———. "El modernismo incógnito." *Quimera* (Revista de Literatura, Barcelona, Spain). Jan. 27, 1983. 8–11.

———. *Modernismo: Supuestos históricos y culturales.* Mexico City: Fondo de cultura económica, 1988.

———. "Los supuestos social-históricos de Modernismo." *Insula* Apr.–May 1987. 485–86, 38–39.

Henríquez Ureña, Max. *Breve historia del modernismo.* Mexico: Fondo de cultura económica, 1954.

Herrera y Reissig, Julio. *El pudor, la cachondez.* Ed. Claudia Giaudrone and Nilo Berriel. Montevideo: Arca, 1992.

Horno-Delgado, Asunción. "Ojos que me reflejan: Poesía autobiográfica de Delmira Agustini." *Letras femeninas* 16.1–2 (1990): 101–12.

Jrade, Cathy L. "Latin America's Search for a Modern Mode of Discourse: Rubén Darío Courts Eulalia." *Recreaciones: Ensayos sobre la obra de Rubén Darío.* Ed. Ivan A. Schulman. Hanover, NH: Ediciones del Norte, 1992. 147–63.

———. *Modernismo, Modernity, and the Development of Spanish American Literature.* Austin: U of Texas P, 1998.

———. "Modernist Poetry." *Cambridge History of Latin American Literature.* Vol. 2. Ed. Roberto González Echevarría and Enrique Puppo-Walker. Cambridge: Cambridge UP, 1996. 7–68.

Kirkpatrick, Gwen. "Delmira Agustini y el 'reino interior de Rodó y Darío." Boulder: Society of Spanish American Studies, 1993.

———. "The Limits of *Modernismo:* Delmira Agustini and Julio Herrera y Reissig." *Romance Quarterly* 36.3 (1989): 307–14.

Lima, Roberto. "Cumbres poéticas del erotismo femenino en Hispanoamérica." *Revista de estudios hispánicos* 18.1 (1984): 41–59.

Machado Bonet, Ofelia. *Delmira Agustini.* Montevideo: Ceibo, 1944.

Marting, Diane E. *The Sexual Woman in Latin American Literature: Dangerous Desires.* Gainesville: UP of Florida, 2001.

Molloy, Silvia. "Dos lecturas del cisne: Rubén Darío y Delmira Agustini." *La sartén por el mango*. Santo Domingo: Corripio, 1985. 57–70.

Monguió, Luis. "De la problemática del modernismo: La crítica y el `cosmopolitismo'." *Revista Iberoamericana* 28 (1962): 75–86.

Moretic, Yerko. "Acerca de las raíces ideológicas del modernismo hispanoamericano." *Philologica Pragensia* 8 (1965): 45–53.

Norat, Gisela. "Vampirismo, sadismo y masoquismo en la poesía de Delmira Agustini." *Lingüística y literatura* 17 (1990): 152–64.

Ovares, Flora, and Margarita Rojas. "Delmira Agustini: La eclosión de los sentidos." *Las poetas del buen amor: La escritura transgresora de Sor Juana Inés de la Cruz, Delmira Agustini, Juana de Ibarbourou, Alfonsina Storni.* Ed. Margarita Rojas, Flora Ovares, and Sonia Mora. Caracas: Monte Avila Latinoamericana, 1991. 85–107.

Paz, Octavio. *Children of the Mire: Modern Poetry from Romanticism to the Avant-Garde*. Cambridge: Harvard UP, 1974.

Pérus, Françoise. *Literatura y sociedad en America Latina: El modernismo*. Mexico City: Siglo veintiuno editores, 1976.

Phillips, Allen W. "Rubén Darío y sus juicios sobre el modernismo." *Revista Iberoamericana* 24.47–48 (1959): 41–64.

Rama, Angel. *The Lettered City*. Trans. and ed. John Charles Chasteen. Durnham: Duke UP, 1996.

———. Prologue. *Aquí la mitad del amor*. Montevideo: Arca, 1966. 7–10.

Real de Azúa, Carlos. "El modernismo literario y las ideologías." *Escritura: Teoría y crítica literarias* 3 (1977): 41–75.

Rodríguez Monegal, Emir. "La Generación del 900." *Número* 2.6–8 (1950): 37–61.

———. *Narradores de esta América*. Montevideo: Alfa, 1969.

———. *La novela latinoamericana*. Caracas: Arte, 1972.

———. *Sexo y poesía en el 900 uruguayo: Los extraños destinos de Roberto y Delmira*. Montevideo: Arca, 1969.

Rojas, Margarita, Flora Ovares, and Sonia Mora. *Las poetas del buen amor: La escritura transgresora de Sor Juana Inés de la Cruz, Delmira Agustini, Juana de Ibarbourou, Alfonsina Storni*. Caracas: Monte Avila Latinoamericana, 1989. 85–107.

Rosenbaum, Sidonia Carmen. *Modern Women Poets of Spanish America*. New York: Hispanic Institute, 1945.

Silva, Clara. *Genio y figura de Delmira Agustini*. Buenos Aires: Eudeba, 1968.

———. *Pasión y gloria de Delmira Agustini: Su vida y su obra*. Buenos Aires: Losada, 1972.

Stephens, Doris T. *Delmira Agustini and the Quest for Transcendence*. Montevideo: Editorial Géminis, 1975.

Tibol, Raquel. *Frida Kahlo: An Open Life*. Trans. Elinor Randall. Albuquerque: U of New Mexico P, 1983.

Valverde, Estela. "Cómo mira a él [D]élmira: La representación del hombre en la poesía de Agustini." *Delmira Agustini y el Modernismo: Nuevas propuestas de género*. Rosario, Argentina: Beatriz Viterbo Editora, 2000: 205–27.

Varas, Patricia. "Máscara vital y liberación estética." *Delmira Agustini: Nuevas penetraciones críticas*. Uruguay Cortazzo. Montevideo: Vintén Editor, 1996. 132–57.

Visca, Arturo Sergio. "Cartas inéditas de Delmira Agustini." *Ensayos sobre literatura uruguaya*. Montevideo: Vinaak, 1975. 201–16.

———. *Correspondencia íntima de Delmira Agustini y tres versiones de "Lo inefable"*. Montevideo: Biblioteca Nacional, 1978.

———. "La poesía de Delmira Agustini." *Delmira Agustini*. Ed. Amanda Berenguer, Arturo Sergio Visca, and José Pedro Díaz. Cuadernos de Literatura, no. 1. Montevideo: Fundación de Cultura Universitaria, 1968. 1–16.

———. "Tres versiones de `Lo inefable' de Delmira Agustini." *Revista de la Biblioteca Nacional* 9 (1975): 9–17.

Yurkievich, Saúl. *Celebración del modernismo*. Barcelona: Tusquets, 1976.

———. "El efecto manifestario, una clave de modernidad." *Recreaciones: Ensayos sobre la obra de Rubén Darío*. Ed. Ivan A. Schulman. Hanover, NH: Ediciones del Norte, 1992. 213–28.

———. "Rubén Darío, precursor de la vanguardia." *Literatura de la emancipación Hispanoamericana y otros ensayos*. Lima: Universidad Nacional Mayor de San Marcos, Dirección Universitaria de Biblioteca y Publicaciones, 1972. 117–31.

Zavala, Iris. Colonialism and Culture. Bloomington: Indiana UP, 1992.

———. "1898, Modernismo, and the Latin American Revolution." *Revista Chicano-Riqueña* 3 (1975) 43–47.

Zum Felde, Alberto. "Carta abierta a Delmira Agustini." *El Día* Feb. 4, 1914: 6, 7.

———. *Crítica de la literatura uruguaya*. Montevideo: M. García, 1921.

———. Prólogo. *Poesías completas de Delmira Agustini*. Buenos Aires: Losada, 1944. 7–37.

———. *Proceso intelectual del Uruguay*. Montevideo: Monteverde, 1930 (2nd ed. 1941; 3rd ed. 1967; 4th ed. 1985; 5th ed. 1987).

DE

El libro blanco (Frágil)

(1907)

FROM

The White Book (Fragile)

(1907)

El poeta leva el ancla

El ancla de oro canta . . . la vela azul asciende
Como el ala de un sueño abierta al nuevo día.
                            Partamos, musa mía!
Ante la prora alegre un bello mar se extiende.

En el oriente claro como un cristal, esplende
El fanal sonrosado de Aurora. Fantasía
Estrena un raro traje lleno de pedrería
Para vagar brillante por las olas.
                                 Ya tiende

La vela azul a Eolo su oriflama de raso . . .
El momento supremo! . . . Yo me estremezco; acaso
Sueño lo que me aguarda en los mundos no vistos? . . .

¿Talvez un fresco ramo de laureles fragantes,
El toisón reluciente, el cetro de diamantes,
El naufragio o la eterna corona de los Cristos? . . .

The Poet Weighs the Anchor

The golden anchor sings . . . the blue sail ascends
Like the wing of a dream open to a new day.
                              Let us part, O Muse!
Before the joyful prow lies a beautiful sea.

In the east, clear as crystal, shines
The rosy lantern of Dawn. Fantasy
Wears a rare gown filled with precious stones
To wander, glorious, by the tides.
                                   The blue sail

To Aeolus now unfolds its satin oriflamme . . .
The supreme moment! I tremble; do I perhaps
Dream of what awaits me in worlds unknown? . . .

Perhaps a fresh bunch of fragrant laurels
The shining Golden Fleece, the diamond scepter,
A shipwreck or the eternal crown of the Christs?

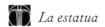 *La estatua*

Miradla, así, sobre el follaje oscuro
Recortar la silueta soberana . . .
¿No parece el retoño prematuro
De una gran raza que será mañana?

Así una raza inconmovible, sana,
Tallada a golpes sobre mármol duro,
De las vastas campañas del futuro
Desalojara a la familia humana!

Miradla así—de hinojos!—en augusta
Calma imponer la desnudez que asusta! . . .—
Dios! . . . Moved ese cuerpo, dadle un alma!
Ved la grandeza que en su forma duerme . . .
¡Vedlo allá arriba, miserable, inerme,
Más pobre que un gusano, siempre en calma!

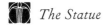 *The Statue*

Behold it, thus, over the dark foliage
Drawing its sovereign silhouette . . .
Does it not seem the premature blossom
Of a race which will live tomorrow?

So an unshakable, robust race
Sculpted with strokes on hard marble,
From the vast campaigns of the future
It will rout the human race.

Behold it, thus—crouched—in imperial
Calm, imposing frightful nakedness!
God! . . . Move that body, give it a soul!
See the greatness that sleeps in its form . . .
See it up there, wretched, defenseless,
Poorer than a worm, forever calm!

 *Una chispa*

Fue un ensueño del fuego
Con luces fascinantes
Y fieras de rubíes tal heridos diamantes;
Rayo de sangre y fuego
Incendió de oro y púrpura todo mi Oriente gris.
Me quedé como ciego . . .
¡Qué luz! . . .—¿Y luego y luego? . . .
—¿Luego? . . . El Oriente gris . . .

A Spark

It was a vision of fire
With fascinating lights
And beasts of ruby like wounded diamonds;
Rays of blood and fire
Inflamed in gold and purple the whole of my gray eastern sky.
I stood as if blind . . .
What a light! . . .—And then, and then?
Then? . . . The gray eastern sky . . .

 *Misterio: Ven . . .*

Ven, oye, yo te evoco.
Extraño amado de mi musa extraña,
Ven, tú, el que meces los enigmas hondos
En el vibrar de las pupilas cálidas.
El que ahondas los cauces de amatista
    De las ojeras cárdenas . . .
    Ven, oye, yo te evoco,
Extraño amado de mi musa extraña!

Ven, tú, el que imprimes un solemne ritmo
Al parpadeo de la tumba helada;
El que dictas los lúgubres acentos
Del decir hondo de las sombras trágicas,
Ven, tú, el poeta abrumador, que pulsas
La lira del silencio: la más rara!
La de las largas vibraciones mudas,
La que se acorda al diapasón del alma!
    Ven, oye, yo te evoco,
Extraño amado de mi musa extraña!

. . . .

Ven, acércate a mí, que en mis pupilas
Se hundan las tuyas en tenaz mirada,
Vislumbre en ellas el sublime enigma
    Del *más allá*, que espanta . . .
Ven . . . acércate más . . . clava en mis labios
    Tus fríos labios de ámbar,
Guste yo en ellos el sabor ignoto
De la esencia enervante de tu alma! . . .

. . . .

    Ven, oye yo te evoco,
Extraño amado de mi musa extraña!

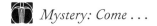 *Mystery: Come . . .*

Come, listen, I call on you,
Strange lover of my strange muse,
Come, you who jumbles the deep enigmas
In the shivering of the warm pupils.
Who hollows out the amethyst riverbed
    Of lived circles under her eyes . . .
    Come, listen, I call on you,
Strange lover of my strange muse!

Come, you, the one who imprints a solemn rhythm
Upon the trembling of the glacial tomb;
The one who sets the dismal tone
Of the deep utterance of tragic shadows.
Come, you, weary poet, who plucks
The lyre of silence: the strangest one!
The one of the long mute vibrations,
Who harmonizes with the sound of the soul!
    Come, listen, I call on you,
Strange lover of my strange muse!

. . . .

Come, come closer to me, that in my pupils
Yours may sink in tenacious sight,
That there may glimmer in them the sublime enigma
    Of the *hereafter,* which frightens . . .
Come . . . come closer to me . . . pierce in my lips
    Your cold lips of amber,
May I try in them the unknown taste
Of the enervating essence of your soul! . . .

. . . .

    Come, listen, I call on you,
Strange lover of my strange muse!

Intima

Yo te diré los sueños de mi vida
En lo más hondo de la noche azul . . .
Mi alma desnuda temblará en tus manos,
Sobre tus hombros pesará mi cruz.

Las cumbres de la vida son tan solas,
Tan solas y tan frías! Yo encerré
Mis ansias en mí misma, y toda entera
Como una torre de marfil me alcé.

Hoy abriré a tu alma el gran misterio;
Ella es capaz de penetrar en mí.
En el silencio hay vértigos de abismo:
Yo vacilaba, me sostengo en ti.

Muero de ensueños; beberé en tus fuentes
Puras y frescas la verdad, yo sé
Que está en el fondo magno de tu pecho
El manantial que vencerá mi sed.

Y sé que en nuestras vidas se produjo
El milagro inefable del reflejo . . .
En el silencio de la noche mi alma
Llega a la tuya como a un gran espejo.

Imagina el amor que habré soñado
En la tumba glacial de mi silencio!
Más grande que la vida, más que el sueño.
Bajo el azur sin fin se sintió preso.

Intimate

I will tell you the dreams of my life
In the deepest corner of the blue night . . .
My naked soul will tremble in your hands,
On your shoulders will weigh my cross.

The peaks of life are so lonesome,
So lonesome and so cold! I confined
My hopes in myself, and vigorous
Like an ivory tower I rose.

Today I will open the great mystery to your soul;
Your soul is capable of penetrating in me.
In the silence there is the vertigo of the abyss:
I hesitated, leaning on you.

I die of reverie; I will drink the truth
In your fountains pure and fresh;
I know in the great vault of your chest
Is the spring that will vanquish my thirst.

And I know that in our lives occurred
The ineffable miracle of reflection . . .
In the silence of the night my soul
Reaches yours like a great mirror.

Imagine the love I must have dreamed of
In the glacial tomb of my silence!
Greater than life, greater than the dream itself
Under the endless azure it felt captured.

Imagina mi amor, amor que quiere
Vida imposible, vida sobrehumana,
Tú que sabes si pesan, si consumen
Alma y sueños de olimpo en carne humana.

Y cuando frente al alma que sentía
Poco el azur para bañar sus alas,
Como un gran horizonte aurisolado
O una playa de luz, se abrió tu alma:

Imagina!! Estrechar vivo, radiante
El imposible! La ilusión vivida!
Bendije a Dios, al sol, la flor, el aire,
La vida toda porque tú eras vida!

 Si con angustia yo compré esta dicha,
Bendito el llanto que manchó mis ojos!
¡Todas las llagas del pasado ríen
Al sol naciente por sus labios rojos!

Ah! tú sabrás mi amor, mas vamos lejos
A través de la noche florecida;
Acá lo humano asusta, acá se oye,
Se ve, se siente, sin cesar la vida.

Vamos más lejos en la noche, vamos
Donde ni un eco repercuta en mí,
Como una flor nocturna allá en la sombra
Yo abriré dulcemente para ti.

Imagine my love, a love that wants
An impossible life, a superhuman life,
You who know how the soul and dreams of Olympus
Weigh upon and consume human flesh.

And when before the soul for which
The azure did little to bathe its wings,
Like a great golden sunned horizon,
Or a beach of life, your soul emerged:

Imagine! To embrace, vivid, radiant
The impossible! The lived illusion!
I blessed God, the sun, the flower, the air
And life itself, because you were life!

If with anguish I have bought this joy
Blessed is the sob that watered my eyes!
All the wounds from the past now laugh
To the rising sun of your red lips!

Ah! you will know my love; but let us go now,
Far away, through the blossoming night;
Here what is human frightens, here one can
Hear, can see, can feel unceasing life.

Let us go farther away into the night, let us go
Where no echo can rebound in me,
Like a nightly flower there in the shadow
I shall softly open for you.

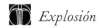 *Explosión*

Si la vida es amor, bendita sea!
Quiero más vida para amar! Hoy siento
Que no valen mil años de la idea
Lo que un minuto azul del sentimiento.

Mi corazón moría triste y lento . . .
Hoy abre en luz como una flor febea;
¡La vida brota como un mar violento
Donde la mano del amor golpea!

Hoy partió hacia la noche, triste, fría
Rotas las alas mi melancolía;
Como una vieja mancha de dolor
En la sombra lejana se deslíe . . .
Mi vida toda canta, besa, ríe!
Mi vida toda es una boca en flor!

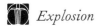 *Explosion*

If life is love, blessed be life!
I want more life to love. Today I feel
A thousand years of an idea are worth not
One beautiful instance of the soul.

My heart was dying, sad and slowly . . .
Today it opens in light like a brilliant flower;
Life springs up like a violent sea
Where the hand of love strikes!

Today, sad and cold, towards the night,
My melancholy—its wings broken—departed.
Like an old stain of grief
In the distant shadows it dissolves . . .
All of my life sings, kisses, laughs!
All my life is a mouth in bloom.

Amor

Yo lo soñé impetuoso, formidable y ardiente;
Hablaba el impreciso lenguaje del torrente;
Era un mar desbordado de locura y de fuego,
Rodando por la vida como un eterno riego.

Luego soñelo triste, como un gran sol poniente
Que dobla ante la noche la cabeza de fuego;
Después rió, y en su boca tan tierna como un ruego,
Sonaba sus cristales el alma de la fuente.

Y hoy sueño que es vibrante, y suave, y riente, y triste,
Que todas las tinieblas y todo el iris viste;
Que, frágil como un ídolo y eterno como Dios,
Sobre la vida toda su majestad levanta:
Y el beso cae ardiendo a perfumar su planta
En una flor de fuego deshojada por dos . . .

Love

I dreamt it impetuous, formidable, and ardent;
It spoke the imprecise language of the torrent,
It was a sea overflowing with madness and fire,
Rolling through life like an eternal fountain.

Afterwards, I dreamt it sad like a great sun setting
That facing the night turns its fiery head;
Then it laughed, and in its mouth as tender as a prayer
The soul of the fountain sounded its crystal.

And today I dream it vibrant and tender, laughing, and sad,
That it dresses all iris and darkness;
That, fragile like an idol and eternal like God,
Its majesty rises above all life:
And the kiss falls in fire to perfume its soles
In a fiery flower plucked by two . . .

 *El intruso*

Amor, la noche estaba trágica y sollozante
Cuando tu llave de oro cantó en mi cerradura;
Luego, la puerta abierta sobre la sombra helante,
Tu forma fue una mancha de luz y de blancura.

Todo aquí lo alumbraron tus ojos de diamante;
Bebieron en mi copa tus labios de frescura,
Y descansó en mi almohada tu cabeza fragante;
Me encantó tu descaro y adoré tu locura.

Y hoy río si tú ríes, y canto si tú cantas;
Y si tú duermes duermo como un perro a tus plantas!
Hoy llevo hasta en mi sombra tu olor de primavera;
Y tiemblo si tu mano toca la cerradura,
Y bendigo la noche sollozante y oscura
Que floreció en mi vida tu boca tempranera!

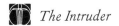 *The Intruder*

Love, the night was tragic and sobbing
When your golden key sang in my lock;
Then, the open door upon the gelid shadow,
Your figure was a stain of light and whiteness.

All was illumined by your diamond eyes;
Your lips of freshness drank in my cup,
And your fragrant head rested on my pillow;
Your impudence fascinated me and I adored your madness.

Today I laugh if you laugh, and I sing if you sing;
And if you sleep I sleep like a dog at your feet!
Today I carry even in my shadow your fragrance of spring;
And I tremble if your hand touches my lock,
And I bless the night sobbing and dark
That in my life your fresh mouth bloomed.

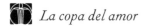 *La copa del amor*

Bebamos juntos en la copa egregia!
Raro licor se ofrenda a nuestras almas.
Abran mis rosas su frescura regia
A la sombra indeleble de tus palmas!

Tú despertaste mi alma adormecida
En la tumba silente de las horas;
A ti la primer sangre de mi vida
¡En los vasos de luz de mis auroras!

Ah! tu voz vino a recamar de oro
Mis lóbregos silencios; tú rompiste
El gran hilo de perlas de mi lloro,
Y al sol naciente mi horizonte abriste.

Por ti, en mi oriente nocturnal, la aurora
Tendió el temblor rosado de su tul;
Así en las sombras de la vida ahora,
Yo te abro el alma como un cielo azul!

¡Ah yo me siento abrir como una rosa!
Ven a beber mis mieles soberanas:
¡Yo soy la copa del amor pomposa
Que engarzará en tus manos sobrehumanas!

La copa erige su esplendor de llama . . .
¡Con qué hechizo en tus manos brillaría!
Su misteriosa exquisitez reclama
Dedos de ensueño y labios de armonía.

De El libro blanco (Frágil) *(*1907*)* / 52

 *The Love Cup*

Let us drink together from the uncommon cup!
Rare liquor is offered to our souls.
May my roses open their royal freshness
Under the indelible shadow of your palms!

You woke my dormant soul
In the silent tomb of the hours;
To you the first blood of my life
In the vases of light of my dawns!

Ah! your voice came to embroider in gold
My lugubrious silence; you broke
The great thread of pearls of my cry,
And to the rising sun you opened my horizon.

For you, in my nocturnal orient, dawn
Spread the shivering pink of its tulle;
So in the shadows of life now,
To you I open my soul like a blue sky!

Ah, I feel I am opening like a rose!
Come drink my sovereign honeys:
My soul is the haughty cup of love
That will be cradled in your superhuman hands!

The cup raises its splendor of flame . . .
With what enchantment would it shine in your hands!
Its mysterious exquisiteness claims
Fingers of reverie, and lips of harmony.

Tómala y bebe, que la gloria dora
El idilio de luz de nuestras almas;
¡Marchítense las rosas de mi aurora
A la sombra indeleble de tus palmas!

Take it and drink, that glory gilds
The idyll of light of our souls:
That the roses of my dawn wither
Under the indelible shadow of your palms!

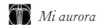 *Mi aurora*

Como un gran sol naciente iluminó mi vida
Y mi alma abrió a beberlo como una flor de aurora;
Amor! Amor! bendita la noche salvadora
En que llamó a mi puerta tu manita florida.

Mi alma vibró en la sombra como arpa sorprendida:
Las aguas del silencio ya abiertas, en la aurora
Cantó su voz potente misteriosa y sonora.
Mi alma lóbrega era una estrella dormida!

Hoy toda la esperanza que yo llorara muerta,
Surge a la vida alada del ave que despierta
Ebria de una alegría fuerte como el dolor;
Y todo luce y vibra, todo despierta y canta,
Como si el palio rosa de su luz viva y santa
Abriera sobre el mundo la aurora de mi amor.

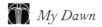 *My Dawn*

Like a great rising sun it illumined my life
And my soul opened to drink it like a flower of dawn;
Love! Love! Blessed be the redeeming night
In which your florid little hand knocked at my door.

My soul pulsated in the shadow like a jarred harp:
The waters of silence already open, at dawn
It sang with its potent voice, mysterious and sonorous.
My gloomy soul was a sleeping star!

Today all the hope that I lamented as dead,
Emerges to the wingèd life of the bird that awakens
Inebriated with a joy strong as sorrow;
And all things shine and pulsate, everything awakens and sings,
As if the rosy canopy of its holy and living light
Opened upon the world the dawn of my love.

 *Desde lejos*

En el silencio siento pasar hora tras hora,
Como un cortejo lento, acompasado y frío . . .
Ah! Cuando tú estás lejos mi vida toda llora
Y al rumor de tus pasos hasta en sueños sonrío.

Yo sé que volverás, que brillará otra aurora
En mi horizonte grave como un ceño sombrío;
Revivirá en mis bosques tu gran risa sonora,
Que los cruzaba alegre como el cristal de un río.

Un día, al encontrarnos tristes en el camino,
Yo puse entre tus manos pálidas mi destino!
¡Y nada de más grande jamás han de ofrecerte!

Mi alma es frente á tu alma como el mar frente al cielo:
Pasarán entre ellas tal la sombra de un vuelo,
La Tormenta y el Tiempo y la Vida y la Muerte!

 *From Far Away*

In silence I feel time passing,
Like a slow parade, cold and rhythmical . . .
Ah! When you are far away my whole life cries
And to the murmur of your steps even in dreams I smile.

I know you will return, that another dawn will shine
In my grave horizon like a somber frown;
There in my forest will live again your great sonorous smile
That gaily crossed it like the glass of a river.

One day, meeting sadly on the path,
In your pale hands I placed my destiny!
And no greater thing will anyone ever offer you!

My soul is before your soul like the sea before the sky:
Between them, like the shadow of a flight,
Storm and time, and life, and death will pass!

DE

Cantos de la mañana

(1910)

FROM

Morning Songs

(1910)

De *"Elegías dulces"*

I

Hoy desde el gran camino, bajo el sol claro y fuerte,
Muda como una lágrima he mirado hacia atrás,
Y tu voz de muy lejos, con un olor de muerte,
Vino a aullarme al oído un triste "¡Nunca más!"

Tan triste que he llorado hasta quedar inerte . . .
¡Yo sé que estás tan lejos que nunca volverás!
No hay lágrimas que laven los besos de la Muerte . . .
—Almas hermanas mías, nunca miréis atrás!

Los pasados se cierran como los ataúdes,
Al Otoño, las hojas en dorados aludes
Ruedan . . . y arde en los troncos la nueva floración . . .

—. . . Las noches son caminos negros de las auroras . . .—
Oyendo deshojarse tristemente las horas
Dulces, hablemos de otras flores al corazón.

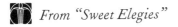 *From "Sweet Elegies"*

I

Today from the great path, under the bright and mighty sun,
Silent like a tear I have looked back,
And your voice from far away, with a scent of death,
Came to howl to my ear a sad "Never again!"

So sad that I have cried until turning numb . . .
I know you are so far away you will never return!
There are no tears able to wash the kisses of death . . .
—Sister souls of mine, never look back!

Past times close like coffins,
In the Fall the leaves in golden cascades
Roll . . . and the new blossoms blaze in the trunks . . .

—. . . The nights are black paths of dawns . . .—
Listening to the sweet hours sadly fading away
Let us talk to the heart about other flowers.

II

Pobres lágrimas mías las que glisan
A la esponja sombría del Misterio,
Sin que abra en flor como una copa cárdena
Tu dolorosa boca de sediento!

Pobre mi corazón que se desangra
Como clepsidra trágica en silencio,
Sin el milagro de inefables bálsamos
En las vendas tremantes de tus dedos!

Pobre mi alma tuya acurrucada
En el pórtico en ruinas del Recuerdo,
Esperando de espaldas a la vida
Que acaso un día retroceda el Tiempo! . . .

II

Poor tears of mine those that slither
Towards the dark sponge of mystery,
Without blooming like a purple cup
Your sorrowful mouth of thirsty man!

My heart, poor, bleeds
Like a tragic and silent water-clock
Without the miracle of ineffable balms
In the trembling bandages of your fingers!

Poor, my soul of yours huddled
At the gates in ruins of memory,
Hoping, its back turned to life,
That perhaps some day time will turn back! . . .

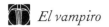 *El vampiro*

En el regazo de la tarde triste
Yo invoqué tu dolor . . . Sentirlo era
Sentirte el corazón! Palideciste
Hasta la voz, tus párpados de cera,

Bajaron . . . y callaste . . . Pareciste
Oír pasar la Muerte . . . Yo que abriera
Tu herida mordí en ella—¿me sentiste?—
Como en el oro de un panal mordiera!

Y exprimí más, traidora, dulcemente
Tu corazón herido mortalmente,
Por la cruel daga rara y exquisita
De un mal sin nombre, hasta sangrarlo en llanto!
Y las mil bocas de mi sed maldita
Tendí a esa fuente abierta en tu quebranto.

. . . .

¿Por qué fui tu vampiro de amargura? . . .
¿Soy flor o estirpe de una especie obscura
Que come llagas y que bebe el llanto?

 *The Vampire*

In the bosom of the sad evening
I called upon your sorrow . . . Feeling it was
Feeling your heart as well. You were pale
Even your voice, your waxen eyelids,

Lowered . . . and remained silent . . . You seemed
To hear death passing by . . . I who had opened
Your wound bit on it—did you feel me?—
As into the gold of a honeycomb I bit!

I squeezed even more treacherously, sweetly
Your heart mortally wounded,
By the cruel dagger, rare and exquisite,
Of a nameless illness, until making it bleed in sobs!
And the thousand mouths of my damned thirst
I offered to that open fountain in your suffering.
. . . .
Why was I your vampire of bitterness?
Am I a flower or a breed of an obscure species
That devours sores and gulps tears?

La noche entró en la sala adormecida
Arrastrando el silencio a pasos lentos . . .
Los sueños son tan quedos que una herida
Sangrar se oiría. Rueda en los momentos

Una palabra insólita, caída
Como una hoja de Otoño . . . Pensamientos
Suaves tocan mi frente dolorida,
Tal manos frescas, ah . . . ¿por qué tormentos

Misteriosos los rostros palidecen
Dulcemente? . . . Tus ojos me parecen
Dos semillas de luz entre la sombra,

Y hay en mi alma un gran florecimiento
Si en mí los fijas; si los bajas, siento
Como si fuera a florecer la alfombra!

The night entered in the sleeping room
Dragging silence with slow steps . . .
The dreams are so silent that a bleeding wound
Could be heard. At moments,

An unusual word rolls, fallen
Like an autumn leaf . . . Tender thoughts
Touch my doleful brow,
Like fresh hands, ah . . . for what mysterious

Torments do faces sweetly
Pale? . . . Your eyes seem to me
Two seeds of light within the shadow,

And there is in my soul a great blossoming
If you fix them upon me; and if you lower them, I feel
As if the carpet were to blossom.

From *Morning Songs* (1910) / 69

La intensa realidad de un sueño lúgubre
Puso en mis manos tu cabeza muerta;
Yo la apresaba como hambriento buitre . . .
Y con más alma que en la Vida trémula
Le sonreía como nadie nunca! . . .
¡Era tan mía cuando estaba muerta!

Hoy la he visto en la Vida, bella, impávida
Como un triunfo estatuario, tu cabeza!
Más frío me dio así que en el idilio
Fúnebre aquel, al estrecharla muerta . . .
¡Y así la lloro hasta agotar mi vida . . .
Así tan viva cuanto me es ajena!

The intense reality of a dismal dream
Placed in my hands your lifeless head;
I clutched it like a ravenous vulture . . .
And with more soul than in life, tremulous,
I smiled to it like no one ever! . . .
It was so much mine when it was dead!

Today I have seen it in life, beautiful, fearless
Like a statuary triumph, your head.
It made me colder so
Than in that funereal idyll,
Embracing it, dead . . .
And thus I mourn it until exhausting my life . . .
Thus as alive as strange to me!

 *La ruptura*

Erase una cadena fuerte como un destino,
Sacra como una vida, sensible como un alma;
La corté con un lirio y sigo mi camino
Con la frialdad magnífica de la Muerte . . . Con calma

Curiosidad mi espíritu se asoma a su laguna
Interior, y el cristal de las aguas dormidas,
Refleja un dios o un monstruo, enmascarado en una
Esfinge tenebrosa suspensa de otras vidas.

 *The Rupture*

There was a chain strong like fate,
Sacred like life, sensitive like a soul;
I cut it with a lily and continue my journey
With the magnificent coldness of death . . . With calm

Curiosity my spirit looks at its inner lake,
And the crystal of the dormant waters,
Reflects a god or a monster, masked in a
Tenebrous sphinx suspended in other lives.

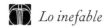 *Lo inefable*

Yo muero extrañamente . . . No me mata la Vida,
No me mata la Muerte, no me mata el Amor;
Muero de un pensamiento mudo como una herida . . .
¿No habéis sentido nunca el extraño dolor

De un pensamiento inmenso que se arraiga en la vida,
Devorando alma y carne, y no alcanza a dar flor?
¿Nunca llevasteis dentro una estrella dormida
Que os abrasaba enteros y no daba un fulgor? . . .

Cumbre de los Martirios! . . . Llevar eternamente,
Desgarradora y árida, la trágica simiente
Clavada en las entrañas como un diente feroz! . . .

Pero arrancarla un día en una flor que abriera
Milagrosa, inviolable! . . . Ah, más grande no fuera
Tener entre las manos la cabeza de Dios!!

De *Cantos de la mañana* (1910) / 74

The Ineffable

I die strangely . . . It is not life that kills me
It is not death that kills me, nor is it love;
I die of a thought, mute as a wound . . .
Have you never felt such a strange pain

Of an immense thought that is rooted in life,
Devouring flesh and soul, and without blooming?
Have you never carried inside a dormant star
That was burning you wholly without shining?

Height of martyrdom! . . . To eternally bear,
Rending and arid, the tragic seed
Pierced in one's entrails like a ferocious fang! . . .

But to uproot it one day in a flower that would bloom
Miraculous, inviolable . . . Ah, it would not be greater
To hold in one's hands the head of God!

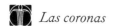 *Las coronas*

. . . ¿Un ensueño entrañable? . . . ¿Un recuerdo profundo? . . .
¡Fue un momento supremo a las puertas de Mundo!

El Destino me dijo maravillosamente:
—Tus sienes son dos vivos engastes soberanos:
Elige una corona, todas van a tu frente!—
Y yo las vi brotar de las fecundas manos,

Floridas y gloriosas, trágicas y brillantes!
Más fría que el marmóreo cadáver de una estatua,
Miré rodar espinas, y flores, y diamantes,
Como el bagaje espléndido de una Quimera fatua.

Luego fue un haz luciente de doradas estrellas;
—Toma!—dijo—son besos del Milagro, entre ellas
Florecerán tus sienes como dos tierras cálidas! . . .

. . . Tal pupilas que mueren, se apagaron rodando . . .
Yo me interné en la Vida, dulcemente, soñando
Hundir mis sienes fértiles entre tus manos pálidas! . . .

 *The Crowns*

. . . A divine illusion? . . . A profound memory? . . .
It was a supreme moment at the gates of the world!

Destiny told me marvelously:
—Your temples are two live royal mountings:
Choose a crown, all go to your brow!—
And I saw them spring from the fertile hands,

Blooming and glorious, tragic and brilliant!
Colder than the marmoreal corpse of a statue,
I saw thorns, and flowers, and diamonds rolling,
Like the splendid accessories of an illusory chimera.

Afterwards it was a shining stream of golden stars;
—Take!—it said—they are kisses of miracle, between them
Like two warm lands your temples will bloom! . . .

. . . Like dying pupils, they rolled away and were extinguished
I walked into life, sweetly, dreaming
To sink my fertile temples into your pale hands! . . .

Las alas

. . . .

Yo tenía . . .

        dos alas! . . .

Dos alas,

Que del Azur vivían como dos siderales

Raíces! . . .

Dos alas,

Con todos los milagros de la vida, la Muerte

Y la Ilusión. Dos alas,

Fulmíneas

Como el velamen de una estrella en fuga;

Dos alas,

Como dos firmamentos

Con tormentas, con calmas y con astros . . .

¿Te acuerdas de la gloria de mis alas? . . .

El áureo campaneo

Del ritmo; el inefable

Matiz atesorando

El Iris todo, mas un Iris nuevo

Ofuscante y divino,

Que adorarán las plenas pupilas del Futuro

(Las pupilas maduras a toda luz!) . . . el vuelo . . .

El vuelo ardiente, devorante y único,

Que largo tiempo atormentó los cielos,

Despertó soles, bólidos, tormentas,

Abrillantó los rayos y los astros;

Y la amplitud: tenían

Calor y sombra para todo el Mundo,

Y hasta incubar un *más allá* pudieron.

 *The Wings*

. . . .

I had . . .

        two wings! . . .

Two wings,

Which of the blue lived like two astral

Roots . . .

Two wings,

With all the miracles of life,

Death,

And illusion. Two wings,

Like lightning

Like the rays of a falling star;

Two wings,

Like two skies

With storms, with calms and with stars . . .

Do you remember the glory of my wings? . . .

The golden bell chime

Of rhythm; the ineffable

Nuance treasuring

The whole iris, but a new iris

Darkening and divine,

Which the wide pupils of the future will adore

(The pupils ripened by full light!) . . . the flight . . .

The eternal flight, devouring and unique,

That long tormented the skies,

Awoke suns, meteorites, storms,

Brightened rays and stars;

And the ampleness: they had

Heat and shade for all the World,

And they were even capable of incubating a *world beyond*.

Un día, raramente
Desmayada a la tierra,
Yo me adormí en las felpas profundas de este bosque . . .
Soñé divinas cosas! . . .
Una sonrisa tuya me despertó, paréceme . . .
Y no siento mis alas! . . .
Mis alas? . . .

—Yo las *vi* deshacerse entre mis brazos . . .
¡Era como un deshielo!

One day, strangely,
Fainted upon the earth,
I fell asleep in the deep velvet of this wood . . .
I dreamt divine things! . . .
A smile of yours awakened me, it seems . . .
And I don't feel my wings! . . .
My wings? . . .

—I *watched* them disappear between my arms
As if melting away!

El nudo

Su idilio fue una larga sonrisa a cuatro labios . . .
En el regazo cálido de rubia primavera
Amáronse talmente que entre sus dedos sabios
Palpitó la divina forma de la Quimera.

En los palacios fúlgidos de las tardes en calma
Hablábanse un lenguaje sentido como un lloro,
Y se besaban hondo hasta morderse el alma! . . .
Las horas deshojáronse como flores de oro,

Y el Destino interpuso sus dos manos heladas . . .
Ah! los cuerpos cedieron, mas las almas trenzadas
Son el más intrincado nudo que nunca fue . . .
En lucha con sus locos enredos sobrehumanos
Las Furias de la vida se rompieron las manos
Y fatigó sus dedos supremos Ananké . . .

The Knot

Their Idyll was a long smile with lips fourfold . . .
In the warm bosom of golden Spring
They loved each other so that between their expert fingers
Palpitated the divine form of chimera.

In the radiant palaces of quiet afternoons
They spoke words that fall on the ear like a sob,
And kissed deeply, so that their souls were consumed!
The hours withered and fell like blossoms of gold.

And fate interposed her two icy hands . . .
Ah, their bodies yielded, but their interwoven souls
Are the most intricate knot there ever was . . .
Struggling with their mad and superhuman liaisons
The furies of life wrought so as to break their hands
And Ananke exhausted her supreme fingers . . .

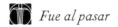 *Fue al pasar*

Yo creí que tus ojos anegaban el mundo . . .
Abiertos como bocas en clamor . . . Tan dolientes
Que un corazón partido en dos trozos ardientes
Parecieron . . . Fluían de tu rostro profundo

Como dos manantiales graves y venenosos . . .
Fraguas a fuego y sombra tus pupilas! . . . tan hondas
Que no sé desde donde me miraban, redondas
Y oscuras como mundos lontanos y medrosos.

¡Ah tus ojos tristísimos como dos galerías
Abiertas al Poniente! . . . Y las sendas sombrías
De tus ojeras donde reconocí mis rastros! . . .

Yo envolví en un gran gesto mi horror como en un velo,
Y me alejé creyendo que cuajaba en el cielo
La medianoche húmeda de tu mirar sin astros!

 *Passing By*

I believed that your eyes were flooding the world . . .
Opened like mouths in clamor . . . So aching
That they seemed a heart broken in two ardent pieces . . .
They were flowing from your enigmatic face

As two springs grave and poisonous . . .
Forges of fire and shadow, your pupils! . . . so deep
That I know not from where they spied me,
Round and obscure like distant and timid worlds.

Ah, your eyes so sad like two galleries
Opened to the west! . . . And the shadowy paths
Of your dark-circled eyes where I traced my path!

I wrapped in a great gesture my horror like in a veil,
And I walked away believing that in the sky there appeared
The moist midnight of your starless gaze!

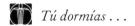 *Tú dormías* . . .

Engastada en mis manos fulguraba
Como extraña presea, tu cabeza;
Yo la ideaba estuches, y preciaba
Luz a luz, sombra a sombra su belleza.

En tus ojos tal vez se concentraba
La vida, como un filtro de tristeza
En dos vasos profundos . . . Yo soñaba
Que era una flor del mármol tu cabeza; . . .

Cuando en tu frente nacarada a luna,
Como un monstruo en la paz de una laguna
Surgió un enorme ensueño taciturno . . .

Ah! tu cabeza me asustó . . . Fluía
De ella una ignota vida . . . Parecía
No sé qué mundo anónimo y nocturno . . .

 *You Were Sleeping* . . .

Encased in my hands like a strange gem
Your head was shining;
For it I imagined jewel-cases, and light for light,
Shadow for shadow, I esteemed its beauty.

In your eyes perhaps life was gathering
Like a filter of sorrow,
In two deep vases . . . I dreamt
Your head was a marble flower . . .

When, in your forehead whitened by moonlight,
Like a monster in the stillness of a lake,
There emerged an enormous, silent dream . . .

Ah! your head frightened me . . . there flowed
From it a hidden life . . . It resembled
I know not what world anonymous and nocturnal . . .

From *Morning Songs* (1910) / 87

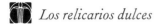

Hace tiempo, algún alma ya borrada fue mía . . .
Se nutrió de mi sombra . . . Siempre que yo quería
El abanico de oro de su risa se abría,

O su llanto sangraba una corriente más;

Alma que yo ondulaba tal una cabellera
Derramada en mis manos . . . Flor del fuego y la cera . . .
Murió de una tristeza mía . . . Tan dúctil era,
Tan fiel, que a veces dudo si pudo ser jamás . . .

De *Cantos de la mañana* (1910) / 88

 *The Sweet Reliquaries*

A time ago, an already forgotten soul belonged to me . . .
It was nurtured by my shadow . . . Whenever I wished,
The golden fan of its laughter would open,

Or its cry would bleed another current;

A soul that I made flow, like long locks
Spilled upon my hands . . . Flower of fire and wax,
It died from a sadness of mine . . . So flexible it was,
So faithful, that at times I doubt if it ever could have been . . .

El raudal

A veces, cuando el amado y yo soñamos en silencio,—un silencio agudo y profundo como el acecho de un sonido insólito y misterioso—siento como si su alma y la mía corrieran lejanamente, por yo no sé qué tierras nunca vistas, en un raudal potente y rumoroso . . .

Torrent

Sometimes, when my beloved one and I dream in silence,—a sharp and deep silence like an unusual and mysterious sound lying in ambush—I feel as if his soul and my soul were running far away, through I know not what lands never seen, in a powerful and roaring torrent . . .

 *Los retratos*

Si os asomarais a mi alma como a una estancia profunda, veríais cuánto la entenebrece e ilumina la intrincada galería de los Desconocidos . . . Figuras incógnitas que, acaso, una sola vez en la vida pasaron por mi lado sin mirarme, y están fijas allá dentro como clavadas con astros . . .

The Portraits

If you looked into my soul as into a large room, you would see how darkened and illumined it is by the intricate gallery of unknown men . . . Unknown figures that perhaps only once in life passed by my side without looking at me, and are fixed deep inside me as if nailed with stars . . .

DE

Los cálices vacíos

(1913)

FROM

The Empty Chalices

(1913)

Debout sur mon orgueil je veux montrer au soir
L'envers de mon manteau endeuillé de tes charmes,
Son mouchoir infini, son mouchoir noir et noir,
Trait á trait, doucement, boira toutes mes larmes.

Il donne des lys blancs á mes roses de flamme
Et des bandeaux de calme á mon front délirant . . .
Que le soir sera bon! . . . Il aura pour moi l'âme
Claire et le corps profond d'un magnifique amant.

De pie, sobre mi orgullo, quiero mostrarte, ¡oh noche!
El revés de mi manto de luto por tu encanto,
Su pañuelo tan negro, infinito pañuelo,
Tan suave, gota a gota, llenaré con mi llanto.

Pondrá sus blancos lirios en mis rosas de llama
Y vendajes de calma en mi sien delirante . . .
¡Será una noche hermosa! . . . Tendrá para mí el alma
Clara y la profundidad del cuerpo de un magnífico amante.

Standing, on my pride, I want to show you, O night!
The reverse of my cloak in mourning for your charm,
His kerchief so black, endless kerchief,
Sweetly, drop by drop, will drink my tears.

He will place white lilies upon my flaming roses
And bandages of calm upon my delirious frown . . .
It will be a beautiful night! It will have, to me, the serene
Soul and the profound body of a magnificent lover.

This poem was originally written in French. In my Spanish critical edition of
Agustini's complete poetry (1999), I included next to the French a Spanish version
of the poem. The English version that appears here is based on both the French
and Spanish versions.

A Eros

Porque haces tu can de la leona
Más fuerte de la Vida, y la aprisiona
La cadena de rosas de tu brazo.

Porque tu cuerpo es la raíz, el lazo
Esencial de los troncos discordantes
Del placer y el dolor, plantas gigantes.

Porque emerge en tu mano bella y fuerte,
Como en broche de místicos diamantes,
El más embriagador lis de la Muerte.

Porque sobre el Espacio te diviso,
Puente de luz, perfume y melodía,
Comunicando infierno y paraíso.

—Con alma fúlgida y carne sombría . . .

To Eros

Because you make life's bravest lioness
Your dog, imprisoning her with the chain
Of roses of your embrace.

Because your body is the root,
The essential tie of divergent stems
Of pleasure and pain, gigantic plants.

Because there emerges from your strong and beautiful hand,
Like a brooch of mystical diamonds,
The most intoxicating lily of death.

Because I glance at you over space,
Bridge of light, perfume and melody,
Connecting inferno and paradise

—With a glowing soul and somber flesh . . .

Tu boca

Yo hacía una divina labor, sobre la roca
Creciente del Orgullo. De la vida lejana,
Algún pétalo vívido me voló en la mañana,
Algún beso en la noche. Tenaz como una loca,
Seguía mi divina labor sobre la roca,

Cuando tu voz que funde como sacra campana
En la nota celeste la vibración humana,
Tendió su lazo de oro al borde de tu boca;

—Maravilloso nido del vértigo, tu boca!
Dos pétalos de rosa abrochando un abismo . . .—

Labor, labor de gloria, dolorosa y liviana;
¡Tela donde mi espíritu se fue tramando el mismo!
Tú quedas en la testa soberbia de la roca,

Y yo caigo, sin fin, en el sangriento abismo!

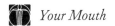 *Your Mouth*

I wrought a divine labor on the Rising
Rock of Pride. Of my past life,
A vivid petal flew away in the morning,
A kiss during the night. Tenacious, as if mad,
I continued my divine labor on the rock.

When your voice, which like a sacred bell melts
In heavenly tone the human vibration,
Extended its golden thread around the edge of your mouth;

. . . Marvelous nest of vertigo, your mouth!
Two petals of rose closing an abyss . . .—

Labor, labor of glory, light and sorrowful;
Cloth where my spirit was weaving itself!
You remain at the proud head of the rock,

And I fall endlessly, into the bloody abyss!

¡Oh tú!

Yo vivía en la torre inclinada
De la Melancolía . . . Las arañas del tedio, las arañas más grises,
En silencio y en gris tejían y tejían.

¡Oh la húmeda torre! . . .
Llena de la presencia
Siniestra de un gran buho,
Como un alma en pena;

Tan mudo que el Silencio en la torre es dos veces;
Tan triste, que sin verlo nos da frío la inmensa
Sombra de su tristeza.

Eternamente incuba un gran huevo infecundo,
Incrustadas las raras pupilas *más allá;*
O caza las arañas del tedio, o traga amargos
Hongos de soledad.

El buho de las ruinas ilustres y las almas
Altas y desoladas!
Náufraga de la Luz yo me ahogaba en la sombra . . .
En la húmeda torre, inclinada a mí misma,
A veces yo temblaba
Del horror de mi sima.

Oh You!

I lived in the leaning tower
Of melancholy . . .
The spiders of tedium, the grayest spiders,
Wove and wove in grayness and silence.

Oh! the dank tower,
Filled with the sinister
Presence of a great owl
Like a soul in torment;

So mute, that the silence in the tower is twofold;
So sad, that without seeing it, we are chilled by the immense
Shadow of its sorrow.

Eternally it incubates a great barren egg,
Its strange pupils fixed on the *hereafter;*
Or hunts the spiders of tedium, or devours bitter
Mushrooms of solitude.

The owl of illustrious ruins and souls
Tall and desolate!
Cast out from the light I drowned in shadows . . .
In the dank tower, leaning over myself,
Sometimes I trembled
From the horror of my abyss.

¡Oh Tú que me arrancaste a la torre más fuerte!

Que alzaste suavemente la sombra como un velo,

Que me lograste rosas en la nieve del alma,

Que me lograste llamas en el mármol del cuerpo;

Que hiciste todo un lago con cisnes, de mi lloro . . .

Tú que en mí todo puedes,

En mí debes ser Dios!

De tus manos yo quiero hasta el Bien que hace mal . . .

Soy el cáliz brillante que colmarás, Señor;

Soy, caída y erguida como un lirio a tus plantas,

Más que tuya, mi Dios!

Perdón, perdón si peco alguna vez, soñando

Que me abrazas con alas ¡todo mío! en el Sol . . .

O you who tore me down from that mightiest tower!
Who gently lifted the shadow like a veil,
Who bore me roses in the snow of my soul,
Who bore me flames in the marble of my body,
Who made a whole lake with swans, of my tears . . .
You who in me are all powerful,
In me you must be God!
From your hands I even seek the good that harms . . .
I am the shining chalice that you will fill, Lord;
Fallen and stiff like a lily, I am at your feet,
I am more than your own, my God!
Forgive me, forgive me, if I should once sin, dreaming
Of your winged embrace, all mine, in the sun . . .

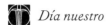

Día nuestro

—La tienda de la noche se ha rasgado hacia Oriente.—
Tu espíritu amanece maravillosamente;
Su luz entra en mi alma como el sol a un vergel . . .

—Pleno sol. Llueve fuego. Tu amor tienta, es la gruta
Afelpada de musgo, el arroyo, la fruta,
La deleitosa fruta madura a toda miel.

—El Angelus. Tus manos son dos alas tranquilas,
Mi espíritu se dobla como un gajo de lilas,
Y mi cuerpo te envuelve . . . tan sutil como un velo.

—El triunfo de la Noche. De tus manos, más bellas,
Fluyen todas las sombras y todas las estrellas,
Y mi cuerpo se vuelve profundo como un cielo!

Our Day

—Night's tent has ripped open to the East.—
Your spirit dawns marvelously;
Its light enters my soul as the sun enters a garden . . .

—The full sun. It rains fire. Your love tempts, it is the cave
Velvety with moss, the stream, the fruit,
The pleasurable fruit fully ripened like honey.

—The Angelus. Your hands are two still wings,
My spirit bends like a branch of lilies,
And my body covers you . . . as subtle as a veil.

—The triumph of the night. From your most beautiful hands,
Flow all the shadows and all the stars,
And my body becomes as deep as the heavens!

Visión

¿Acaso fue en un marco de ilusión,
En el profundo espejo del deseo,
O fue divina y simplemente en vida
Que yo te vi velar mi sueño la otra noche?

En mi alcoba agrandada de soledad y miedo,
Taciturno á mi lado apareciste
Como un hongo gigante, muerto y vivo,
Brotado en los rincones de la noche
Húmedos de silencio,
Y engrasados de sombra y soledad.

Te inclinabas a mí supremamente,
Como a la copa de cristal de un lago
Sobre el mantel de fuego del desierto;
Te inclinabas a mí, como un enfermo
De la vida a los opios infalibles
Y a las vendas de piedra de la Muerte;
Te inclinabas a mí como el creyente
A la oblea de cielo de la hostia . . .
—Gota de nieve con sabor de estrellas
Que alimenta los lirios de la Carne,
Chispa de Dios que estrella los espíritus—.
Te inclinabas a mí como el gran sauce
De la Melancolía
A las hondas lagunas del silencio;
Te inclinabas a mí como la torre
De mármol del Orgullo,
Minada por un monstruo de tristeza,
A la hermana solemne de su sombra . . .
Te inclinabas a mí como si fuera
Mi cuerpo la inicial de tu destino
En la página oscura de mi lecho;

Vision

Was it perhaps illusion,
Framed in the deep mirror of desire,
Or was it in life, simply and divinely
That I saw you watching over me in my sleep the other night?

In my chamber enlarged by solitude and fear
Silent you appeared by my side
Like a giant mushroom, alive and dead,
Springing from the corners of the night,
Humid with silence,
And greased with shadow and solitude.

You leaned over me, supremely,
As over the crystal cup of a lake
Upon the fiery shroud of the desert;
You leaned over me, as someone sick
Of life does over the infallible opiates
And over the stone bandages of death.
You leaned over me as the believer
Over the heavenly sacrament of the host . . .
—A drop of snow with the taste of stars
That feeds the lilies of the flesh,
A spark of God that shatters the spirits—.
You leaned over me as the great willow
Of melancholy
Over the deep waters of silence;
You leaned over me as the
Marble tower of pride,
Undermined by a monster of sadness,
Over the solemn sister of its shadow . . .
You leaned over me as if
My body were the initial letter of your destiny
On the obscure page of my bed;

Te inclinabas a mí como al milagro
De una ventana abierta al más allá.

¡Y te inclinabas más que todo eso!

   Y era mi mirada una culebra
Apuntada entre zarzas de pestañas,
Al cisne reverente de tu cuerpo.
Y era mi deseo una culebra
Glisando entre los riscos de la sombra
A la estatua de lirios de tu cuerpo!

   Tú te inclinabas más y más . . . y tanto,
Y tanto te inclinaste,
Que mis flores eróticas son dobles,
Y mi estrella es más grande desde entonces.
Toda tu vida se imprimió en mi vida . . .

   Yo esperaba suspensa el aletazo
Del abrazo magnífico; un abrazo
De cuatro brazos que la gloria viste
De fiebre y de milagro, será un vuelo!
Y pueden ser los hechizados brazos
Cuatro raíces de una raza nueva:

   Y esperaba suspensa el aletazo
Del abrazo magnífico . . .
Y cuando,
Te abrí los ojos como un alma, y vi
Que te hacías atrás y te envolvías
En yo no sé qué pliegue inmenso de la sombra!

You leaned over me as towards the miracle
Of a window open to the hereafter.

And you leaned over me still more than all of that!

   And my gaze was a snake
Aimed between eyelash brambles,
Towards the reverent swan of your body,
And a snake was my desire
Crawling among the crags of the shadow
Towards the statues of lilies of your body.

   You leaned more and more . . . so much,
So much you leaned,
That my erotic flowers are doubled,
And my star is greater ever since.
All your life was impressed on my life . . .

   Suspenseful I awaited the fluttering wing
Of the magnificent embrace; an embrace
Of four arms that glory adorns
With fever and miracle, it might soar!
And the bewitched arms might be
Four roots of a new race.

   Suspenseful I awaited the wing's flutter
Of the magnificent embrace . . .
And when,
I opened my eyes to you as a soul, I saw
That you faded away and wrapped yourself
In I know not what immense fold of the shadows!

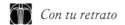 *Con tu retrato*

Yo no sé si mis ojos o mis manos
Encendieron la vida en tu retrato;
Nubes humanas, rayos sobrehumanos,
Todo tu *Yo* de emperador innato

Amanece a mis ojos, en mis manos!
Por eso, toda en llamas, yo desato
Cabellos y alma para tu retrato,
Y me abro en flor! . . . Entonces, soberanos

De la sombra y la luz, tus ojos graves
Dicen grandezas que yo sé y tú sabes . . .
Y te dejo morir . . . Queda en mis manos
Una gran mancha lívida y sombría . . .
Y renaces en mi melancolía
Formado de astros fríos y lejanos!

With Your Portrait

I don't know if my eyes or my hands
Sparked life in your portrait;
Human clouds, superhuman rays,
All your *I* of innate emperor

Rises to my eyes, in my hands.
For that, all in flames, I unbind
Hair and soul for your portrait,
And I open in bloom! . . . Then, sovereign,

Of shadow and light, your grave eyes
Say great things that I know and you know . . .
And I let you die . . . In my hands remains
A great stain, livid and somber . . .
And in my melancholy you are born again
Formed by cold and remote stars!

 *Otra estirpe*

Eros yo quiero guiarte, Padre ciego . . .
Pido a tus manos todopoderosas,
Su cuerpo excelso derramado en fuego
Sobre mi cuerpo desmayado en rosas!

La eléctrica corola que hoy desplego
Brinda el nectario de un jardin de Esposas;
Para sus buitres en mi carne entrego
Todo un enjambre de palomas rosas!

Da a las dos sierpes su abrazo, crueles,
Mi gran tallo febril . . . Absintio, mieles,
Viérteme de sus venas, de su boca . . .

¡Así tendida soy un surco ardiente,
Donde puede nutrirse la simiente,
De otra Estirpe sublimemente loca!

 *Another Lineage*

Eros, I want to guide you, blind Father . . .
From your almighty hands I ask for
His sublime body spilled in fire
Upon my body faint in roses!

The electric corolla that I now open
Offers the nectary of a garden of wives;
To his vultures in my flesh I offer
A whole swarm of roseate doves.

Give to the two cruel serpents of his embrace
My great feverish stem . . . Absinth, honeys,
Spill on me from his veins, from his mouth . . .

Thus lying I am an ardent furrow
Where can be nurtured the seed
Of another lineage sublimely mad!

 *El surtidor de oro*

Vibre, mi musa, el surtidor de oro
La taza rosa de tu boca en besos;
De las espumas armoniosas surja
Vivo, supremo, misterioso, eterno,
El amante ideal, el esculpido
En prodigios de almas y de cuerpos;
Debe ser vivo a fuerza de soñado,
Que sangre y alma se me va en los sueños;
Ha de nacer a deslumbrar la Vida,
Y ha de ser un dios nuevo!
Las culebras azules de sus venas
Se nutren de milagro en mi cerebro . . .

Selle, mi musa, el surtidor de oro
La taza rosa de tu boca en besos;
El amante ideal, el esculpido
En prodigios de almas y de cuerpos,
Arraigando las uñas extrahumanas
En mi carne, solloza en mis ensueños:
—Yo no quiero más Vida que tu vida,
Son en ti los supremos elementos;
Déjame bajo el cielo de tu alma,
En la cálida tierra de tu cuerpo!—
—Selle, mi musa, el surtidor de oro
La taza rosa de tu boca en besos!

De *Los cálices vacíos* (1913) / 116

The Golden Fountain

O Muse, let the golden fountain vibrate
The rosy cup of your mouth with kisses;
From the harmonious foams let spring forth
Live, supreme, mysterious, eternal
The ideal lover, the one sculpted
In prodigies of souls and bodies;
He must be alive by force of dreaming,
As blood and soul are taken from me in my dreams;
He must be born to dazzle Life,
And he must be a new god!
The blue serpents of his veins
Are nourished by miracle in my mind . . .

O Muse, let the golden fountain seal
The rosy cup of your mouth with kisses;
The ideal lover, the one sculpted
In prodigies of souls and bodies,
Rooting his superhuman nails
In my flesh, he sobs in my reveries:
—I want no other life than your life,
In you exist the supreme elements;
Leave me under the sky of your soul,
In the warm soil of your body!—
—O Muse, let the golden fountain seal
The rosy cup of your mouth with kisses!

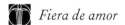 *Fiera de amor*

Fiera de amor, yo sufro hambre de corazones.
De palomos, de buitres, de corzos o leones,
No hay manjar que más tiente, no hay más grato sabor,
Había ya estragado mis garras y mi instinto,
Cuando erguida en la casi ultratierra de un plinto,
Me deslumbró una estatua de antiguo emperador.

Y crecí de entusiasmo; por el tronco de piedra
Ascendió mi deseo como fulmínea hiedra
Hasta el pecho, nutrido en nieve al parecer;
Y clamé al imposible corazón . . . la escultura
Su gloria custodiaba serenísima y pura,
Con la frente en Mañana y la planta en Ayer.

Perenne mi deseo, en el tronco de piedra
Ha quedado prendido como sangrienta hiedra;
Y desde entonces muerdo soñando un corazón
De estatua, presa suma para mi garra bella;
No es ni carne ni mármol: una pasta de estrella
Sin sangre, sin calor y sin palpitación . . .

Con la esencia de una sobrehumana pasión!

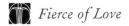 *Fierce of Love*

Fierce of love, I suffer hunger for hearts.
Of pigeons, of vultures, of roe deer or lions,
There is no prey more tempting, there is no taste more pleasing;
I had already dulled my claws and my instinct,
When, erected, in an almost unreal plinth,
I was captivated by a statue of an ancient emperor.

And I grew in enthusiasm; along the stem of stone
My desire ascended like a fulmineous ivy
Up to his chest, nurtured seemingly in snow;
I shouted to the impossible heart . . . the sculpture
Most serene and pure, guarding its glory
With its brow in the future
And its feet in the past.

Perennial was my desire, in the stem of stone
It has remained affixed like bloody ivy;
And ever since I gnaw in my dreams at the heart
Of a statue, exquisite prey for my beautiful claw;
It is neither flesh nor marble: the dough of a star
With no blood, with no warmth and with no heartbeat . . .

With the essence of a superhuman passion!

Ceguera

Me abismo en una rara ceguera luminosa
Un astro, casi un alma, me ha velado la Vida.
¿Se ha prendido en mí como brillante mariposa,
O en su disco de luz he quedado prendida?

  No sé . . .
  Rara ceguera que me borras el mundo,
Estrella, casi alma, con que asciendo o me hundo:
Dame tu luz y vélame eternamente el mundo!

Blindness

I fall into a strange luminous blindness,
A star, almost a soul, has hidden life from me.
Has it been caught in me like a brilliant butterfly,
Or in its halo of light have I been seized?

I know not . . .
Rare blindness that erases the world,
Star, almost a soul, with which I rise or I fall:
Give me your light and forever veil my world!

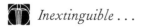 *Inextinguible . . .*

O tú que duermes tan hondo que no despiertas!
Milagrosas de vivas, milagrosas de muertas,
Y por muertas y vivas eternamente abiertas,

Alguna noche en duelo yo encuentro tus pupilas

Bajo un trapo de sombra o una blonda de luna.
Bebo en ellas la calma como en una laguna.
Por hondas, por calladas, por buenas, por tranquilas

Un lecho o una tumba parece cada una.

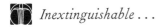 *Inextinguishable . . .*

O you who sleep so deep that you do not wake!
Miraculous when alive, miraculous when dead,
And for dead and alive eternally open,

Some night in mourning I find your pupils

Under a cloth of shadow or a lace of moon.
I drink in them the calm as in a pond
For profound, for silent, for good, for tranquil

A bed or a tomb each seems to be.

Nocturno

Engarzado en la noche el lago de tu alma,
Diríase una tela de cristal y de calma
Tramada por las grandes arañas del desvelo.

Nata de agua lustral en vaso de alabastros;
Espejo de pureza que abrillantas los astros
Y reflejas la sima de la Vida en un cielo!...

Yo soy el cisne errante de los sangrientos rastros,
Voy manchando los lagos y remontando el vuelo.

 *Nocturnal*

Mounted in the night is the lake of your soul,
A cloth, one would say, of crystal and calm
Woven by the large spiders of wakefulness.

A skim of sacred water in alabaster vases;
A mirror of purity that brightens the stars
And reflects the abyss of life in a sky! . . .

I am the wandering swan of the bloody trails,
I go staining the lakes and rising up in flight.

El cisne

Pupila azul de mi parque
Es el sensitivo espejo
De un lago claro, muy claro! . . .
Tan claro que a veces creo
Que en su cristalina página
Se imprime mi pensamiento.

Flor del aire, flor del agua,
Alma del lago es un cisne
Con dos pupilas humanas,
Grave y gentil como un príncipe;
Alas lirio, remos rosa . . .
Pico en fuego, cuello triste
Y orgulloso, y la blancura
Y la suavidad de un cisne . . .

El ave cándida y grave
Tiene un maléfico encanto;
—Clavel vestido de lirio,
Trasciende a llama y milagro! . . .
Sus alas blancas me turban
Como dos cálidos brazos;
Ningunos labios ardieron
Como su pico en mis manos;
Ninguna testa ha caído
Tan lánguida en mi regazo;
Ninguna carne tan viva,
He padecido o gozado:
Viborean en sus venas
Filtros dos veces humanos!

The Swan

  Blue pupil of my park
In the sensitive mirror
Of a clear lake, very clear . . .
So clear that sometimes I believe
Upon its crystalline page
My thoughts are printed.

  Flower of the air, flower of the water,
The soul of the lake is a swan
With two human pupils,
Formal and gentle as a prince;
Lily wings, rosy sculls . . .
A fiery beak, a sad
And proud neck, and the whiteness
And the softness of a swan . . .

  The candid and solemn bird
Has a wicked charm;
—A carnation dressed in lily,
It transcends in flame and miracle . . .
His white wings disturb me
Like two warm arms;
  No lips have ever burned
As his beak in my hands;
No head has ever fallen
So languorous into my lap;
No flesh so alive
Have I ever suffered or enjoyed;
In his veins crawl
Philters two times human.

Del rubí de la lujuria
Su testa está coronada;
Y va arrastrando el deseo
En una cauda rosada . . .

Agua le doy en mis manos
Y él parece beber fuego;
Y yo parezco ofrecerle
Todo el vaso de mi cuerpo . . .

Y vive tanto en mis sueños,
Y ahonda tanto en mi carne,
Que a veces pienso si el cisne
Con sus dos alas fugaces,
Sus raros ojos humanos
Y el rojo pico quemante,
Es sólo un cisne en mi lago
O es en mi vida un amante . . .

Al margen del lago claro
Yo le interrogo en silencio . . .
Y el silencio es una rosa
Sobre su pico de fuego . . .
Pero en su carne me habla
Y yo en mi carne le entiendo.
—A veces ¡toda! soy alma;
Y a veces ¡toda! soy cuerpo.—
Hunde el pico en mi regazo
Y se queda como muerto . . .
Y en la cristalina página,
En el sensitivo espejo
Del lago que algunas veces
Refleja mi pensamiento,
El cisne asusta de rojo,
Y yo de blanca doy miedo!

With the ruby of lust
His head is crowned;
And he goes dragging desire
In a rosy cape . . .

In my hands I give him water
And fire he seems to drink;
And I seem to offer him
The whole vase of my body . . .

And he lives so much in my dreams,
And sinks so deep in my flesh
That sometimes I wonder whether the swan,
With his two fleeting wings,
His rare human eyes
And the red burning beak
Is only a swan in my lake
Or a lover in my life . . .

At the edge of the clear lake
I query him in silence . . .
And the silence is a rose
Over his fiery beak . . .
But in his flesh he speaks to me
And I in my flesh understand him.
 —Sometimes, I am all soul;
And sometimes, I am all body.—
He buries his beak in my lap
And remains still as if dead . . .
And on the crystalline page,
In the sensitive mirror
Of the lake that sometimes
Reflects my thoughts,
The swan is frightfully red,
And I dreadful in my whiteness!

Plegaria

—Eros: acaso no sentiste nunca
Piedad de las estatuas?
Se dirían crisálidas de piedra
De yo no sé qué formidable raza
En una eterna espera inenarrable.
Los cráteres dormidos de sus bocas
Dan la ceniza negra del Silencio,
Mana de las columnas de sus hombros
La mortaja copiosa de la Calma,
Y fluye de sus órbitas la noche;
Víctimas del Futuro o del Misterio,
En capullos terribles y magníficos
Esperan a la Vida o a la Muerte.
Eros: acaso no sentiste nunca
Piedad de las estatuas?—
Piedad para las vidas
Que no doran a fuego tus bonanzas
Ni riegan o desgajan tus tormentas;
Piedad para los cuerpos revestidos
Del arminio solemne de la Calma,
Y las frentes en luz que sobrellevan
Grandes lirios marmóreos de pureza,
Pesados y glaciales como témpanos;
Piedad para las manos enguantadas
De hielo, que no arrancan
Los frutos deleitosos de la Carne
Ni las flores fantásticas del alma;
Piedad para los ojos que aletean
Espirituales párpados:
Escamas de misterio,
Negros telones de visiones rosas . . .
¡Nunca ven nada por mirar tan lejos!
Piedad para las pulcras cabelleras

Entreaty

Eros: have you ever felt
Piety for the statues?
One would say they are chrysalides of stone
Of I know not what formidable lineage
In an eternal, unspeakable wait.
The sleeping craters of their mouths
Give the black ash of silence,
From the columns of his shoulders
Emanates the copious shroud of calm,
And from the hollows of their eyes the night flows;
Victims of the Future or the Mystery,
In terrible and magnificent blooms
Await life or death.
Eros: have you ever felt piety for the statues?
Piety for the lives
That with fire guild not your calms
Nor besprinkle or break off your storms;
Piety for the bodies clad
In the solemn ermine of calm,
And the lighted foreheads that bear
Great marmoreal lilies of purity,
Heavy and glacial like icebergs;
Piety for the hands gloved
With ice, which pick not
The pleasurable fruits of the flesh
Nor the fanciful flowers of the soul;
Piety for the eyes that bat
Spiritual eyelids:
Scales of mystery,
Black shrouds of rosy visions . . .
They never see anything no matter how far they look!
Piety for the fine locks

—Místicas aureolas—
Peinadas como lagos
Que nunca airea el abanico negro,
Negro y enorme de la tempestad;
Piedad para los ínclitos espíritus
Tallados en diamante,
Altos, claros, extáticos
Pararrayos de cúpulas morales;
Piedad para los labios como engarces
Celestes donde fulge
Invisible la perla de la Hostia;
—Labios que nunca fueron,
Que no apresaron nunca
Un vampiro de fuego
Con más sed y más hambre que un abismo.—

Piedad para los sexos sacrosantos
Que acoraza de una
Hoja de viña astral la Castidad;
Piedad para las plantas imantadas
De eternidad que arrastran
Por el eterno azul
Las sandalias quemantes de sus llagas;
Piedad, piedad, piedad
Para todas las vidas que defiende
De tus maravillosas intemperies
El mirador enhiesto del Orgullo:

Apúntales tus soles o tus rayos!

Eros: acaso no sentiste nunca
Piedad de las estatuas? . . .

—mystical halos—
Combed as lakes
Never aired by the black fan,
The black and enormous fan of the tempest;
Piety for the illustrious spirits
Carved in diamond,
Tall, clear, ecstatic
Lightning rods of moral domes;
Piety for the lips like celestial gem mountings
Where shines
Invisible the pearl of the host;
—lips that were never,
That never captured
A vampire of fire
With more thirst and more hunger than an abyss—.
Piety for the sacred sexes
That chastity ironclads
With a leaf of an astral vine;
Piety for the magnetized soles
Of eternity which drag
Through the eternal azure
The burning sandals of their wounds;
Piety, piety, piety
For all the lives that are defended
From your spectacular elements by
The erect tower of pride:

Aim your sunbeams or your thunderbolts at them!

Eros: have you ever felt
Piety for the statues?

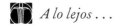 *A lo lejos . . .*

Tu vida viuda enjoyará aquel día . . .
En la gracia silvestre de la aldea
Era una llaga tu perfil arcano;
Insólito, alarmante sugería
El esmalte de espléndida presea
Sobre un pecho serrano.

Por boca de la abierta ventana suspiraba
Toda la huerta en flor, era por puro
Toda la aldea el cuarto asoleado;
¿Recuerdas? . . . Sobre mí se proyectaba,
Más mortal que tu sombra sobre el muro,
Tu solemne tristeza de extraviado . . .
Tus manos alargadas de tenderse al Destino,
Todopalidecidas de amortajar quimeras,
Parecían tocarme de muy lejos . . .
Tus ojos eran un infinito camino
Y crecían las lunas nuevas de tus ojeras;
En solo un beso nos hicimos viejos . . .

—¡Oh beso! . . . flor de cuatro pétalos . . . dos de Ciencia
Y dos iluminados de inocencia . . .
El cáliz una sima embriagante y sombría.—
Por un milagro de melancolía,
Mármol ó bronce me rompí en tu mano
Derramando mi espíritu, tal un pomo de esencia.

Tu vida viuda enjoyará aquel día . . .
Mi nostalgia ha pintado tu perfil Wagneriano
Sobre el velo tremendo de la ausencia.

At a Distance . . .

Your widow life will adorn that day in jewels . . .
In the wild charm of the village
Your arcane profile was a wound;
Unusual, alarming, it suggested
The enamel of a precious gem
Upon a mountainous breast.

Through the mouth of the open window sighed
All the orchard in bloom, and the sunny room
Was itself all the village;
Remember? . . . Upon me was projected,
More mortal than your shadow on the wall,
Your solemn sorrow of one gone astray . . .
Your hands, elongated by grasping toward fate,
All pale by trying to shroud dreams,
Seemed to touch me from a distance . . .
Your eyes were an infinite path
And new moons grew out below your eyes;
In only one kiss we became old . . .

—Oh, kiss! . . . flower of four petals . . . two of knowledge
And two illumined by innocence . . .
The chalice an abyss, enrapturing and somber.—
By a miracle of melancholy,
Marble or brass I shattered in your hand
Spilling my spirit, like a pomander of essence.

Your widowed life will adorn that day in jewels . . .
My nostalgia has painted your Wagnerian profile
Upon the tremendous veil of absence.

DE

Los Astros del abismo

(1924)

FROM

The Stars of the Abyss

(1924)

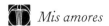 *Mis amores*

Hoy han vuelto.
Por todos los senderos de la noche han venido
A llorar en mi lecho.
¡Fueron tantos, son tantos!
Yo no sé cuáles viven, yo no sé cuál ha muerto.
Me lloraré yo misma para llorarlos todos.
La noche bebe el llanto como un pañuelo negro.

Hay cabezas doradas a sol, como maduras . . .
Hay cabezas tocadas de sombra y de misterio,
Cabezas coronadas de una espina invisible,
Cabezas que sonrosa la rosa del ensueño,
Cabezas que se doblan a cojines de abismo,
Cabezas que quisieran descansar en el cielo,
Algunas que no alcanzan a oler a primavera,
Y muchas que trascienden a las flores de invierno.
Todas esas cabezas me duelen como llagas . . .
Me duelen como muertos . . .
¡Ah! . . . y los ojos . . . los ojos me duelen más: ¡son dobles! . . .
Indefinidos, verdes, grises, azules, negros,
Abrasan si fulguran,
Son caricias, dolor constelación, infierno.
Sobre toda su luz, sobre todas sus llamas,
Se iluminó mi alma y se templó mi cuerpo.
Ellos me dieron sed de todas esas bocas . . .
De todas estas bocas que florecen mi lecho:
Vasos rojos o pálidos de miel o de armargura
Con lises de armonía o rosas de silencio,
De todos estos vasos donde bebí la vida,
De todos estos vasos donde la muerte bebo . . .
El jardín de sus bocas venenoso, embriagante,
En donde respiraba *sus* almas y *sus* cuerpos,

 *My Loves*

Today they have returned.
Through all paths of the night they have come
To cry on my bed.
They were so many, they are so many!
I know not which are alive, I know not who has died.
I myself shall melt in sobs to cry for all of them.
The night drinks the tears like a black kerchief.

There are heads gilded by the sun, as if ripened . . .
There are heads touched by shadow and mystery,
Heads crowned by an invisible thorn,
Heads that the rose of reverie makes blush.
Heads that bend over cushions of the abyss,
Heads that would wish to rest in the sky,
Some that never succeed in smelling of spring,
And many that smell of the flowers of winter.
All those heads hurt me like wounds . . .
They hurt me like the dead . . .
Ah . . . and the eyes . . . the eyes hurt me even more: they are double!
Ill-defined, green, gray, blue, black
They burn as they shine,
They are caresses, grief, stars, hell.
Upon all their light, upon all their flames,
My soul was illuminated and my body tempered.
They made me thirst for all those mouths . . .
For all those mouths that flower in my bed:
Pale or red vases of honey or bitterness
With lilies of harmony or roses of silence,
From all those vases where I drank of life,
From all those vases where of death I drink . . .
The venomous and intoxicating garden of their mouths
Where I breathed in *their* souls and *their* bodies,

Humedecido en lágrimas
Ha cercado mi lecho . . .

Y las manos, las manos colmadas de destinos
Secretos y alhajadas de anillos de misterio . . .
Hay manos que nacieron con guantes de caricia,
Manos que están colmadas de la flor del deseo,
Manos en que se siente un puñal nunca visto,
Manos en que se ve un intangible cetro;
Pálidas o morenas, voluptuosas o fuertes,
En todas, todas ellas, puede engarzar un sueño.

    Con tristeza de almas,
    Se doblegan los cuerpos,
    Sin velos, santamente
    Vestidos de deseo.
Imanes de mis brazos, panales de mi entraña
Como a invisible abismo se inclinan a mi lecho . . .

¡Ah, entre todas las manos yo he buscado tus manos!
Tu boca entre las bocas, tu cuerpo entre los cuerpos,
De todas las cabezas yo quiero tu cabeza,
De todos esos ojos, ¡tus ojos solos quiero!
Tú eres el más triste, por ser el más querido,
Tú has llegado el primero por venir de más lejos . . .

¡Ah, la cabeza oscura que no he tocado nunca
Y las pupilas claras que miré tanto tiempo!
Las ojeras que ahondamos la tarde y yo inconscientes,
La palidez extraña que doblé sin saberlo,
    Ven a mí: mente a mente;
    Ven a mí: ¡cuerpo a cuerpo!
Tú me dirás qué has hecho de mi primer suspiro,
Tú me dirás qué has hecho del sueño de aquel beso . . .

Moistened in tears,
Has circled my bed . . .

And the hands, the hands filled with secret
Destinies, and adorned with rings of mystery . . .
There are hands that were born with gloves of caresses
Hands filled with the bloom of desire,
Hands in which one feels a dagger never seen,
Hands in which one can see an intangible scepter;
Pale or dark, voluptuous or powerful,
In all, in all of them, a dream can be cupped.

   With sadness of souls
   The bodies bend
   Unveiled, saintly
   Dressed in desire.
Magnets of my arms, honeycombs of my bosom
As to an invisible abyss they lean towards my bed . . .

Ah, among all hands I have sought your hands!
Your mouth among the mouths, your body among the bodies;
Of all the heads I want your head,
Of all those eyes, your eyes only I want!
You are the saddest, for being the most beloved,
You have arrived first, for coming the farthest . . .

Ah, the dark head I have never touched
And the light pupils I gaze at for so long!
The dark-circled eyes the evening and I deepened unwittingly,
The strange paleness I bent without knowing.
   Come to me: mind to mind;
   Come to me: body to body!
You will tell me what you have made of my first sigh,
You will tell me what you have made of the dream of that kiss . . .

Me dirás si lloraste cuando te dejé solo . . .
    ¡Y me dirás si has muerto! . . .

    Si has muerto,
Mi pena enlutará la alcoba lentamente,
Y estrecharé tu sombra hasta apagar mi cuerpo.
Y en el silencio ahondado de tiniebla,
Y en la tiniebla ahondada de silencio,
Nos velará llorando, llorando hasta morirse
    Nuestro hijo: el recuerdo.

You will tell me if you cried when I left you alone . . .
    And you will tell me if you have died! . . .

    If you have died,
My grief will slowly dress the chamber in mourning
And I will embrace your shadow until I have smothered my body
And in the silence deepened in darkness
And in the darkness deepened in silence,
He will weep over us, weeping until death,
    Our son: memory.

Tu amor, esclavo, es como un sol muy fuerte:
Jardinero de oro de la vida,
Jardinero de fuego de la muerte,
En el carmen fecundo de mi vida.

Pico de cuervo con olor de rosas,
Aguijón enmelado de delicias
Tu lengua es. Tus manos misteriosas
Son garras enguantadas de caricias.

Tus ojos son mis medianoches, crueles,
Panales negros de malditas mieles
Que se desangran en mi acerbidad;

Crisálida de un vuelo del futuro,
Es tu abrazo magnífico y oscuro
Torre embrujada de mi soledad.

Your love, slave, is like a burning sun:
Golden gardener of life,
Fiery gardener of death,
In the fertile garden of my life

A raven's beak with the fragrance of roses
A honeyed sting of delights
Is your tongue. Your mysterious hands
Are claws gloved with caresses.

Your eyes are midnights, cruel,
Black honeycombs of cursèd honeys
That bleed upon my bitterness;

Chrysalis of a future flight,
Is your dark and magnificent embrace,
Bewitched tower of my solitude.

El arroyo

¿Te acuerdas? ... El arroyo fue la serpiente buena ...
Fluía triste y triste como un llanto de ciego,
Cuando en las piedras grises donde arraiga la pena,
Como un inmenso lirio, se levantó tu ruego.

Mi corazón, la piedra más gris y más serena,
Despertó en la caricia de la corriente, y luego
Sintió cómo la tarde, con manos de agarena,
Prendía sobre él una rosa de fuego.

Y mientras la serpiente del arroyo blandía
El veneno divino de la melancolía,
Tocada de crepúsculo me abrumó tu cabeza,

La coroné de un beso fatal; en la corriente
Vi pasar un cadáver de fuego ... Y locamente
Me derrumbó en tu abrazo profundo la tristeza.

 *The Stream*

Remember? . . . The stream was the kind serpent . . .
It flowed sadly and sadly like the cry of a blind man,
When in the gray stones where sorrow is rooted,
Like an immense lily, there arose your prayer.

My heart, the grayest and most serene stone,
Awoke in the caress of the stream, and then
It felt like the evening, with hands of a Mohammedan
There hung from it a rose of fire.

And while the serpent of the stream brandished
The divine poison of melancholy,
Touched by the sunset your head overwhelmed me,

I crowned it with a fatal kiss; in the current
I saw a corpse of fire passing by . . . And madly
In your deep embrace, sorrow cast me to the ground.

 *Por tu musa*

Cuando derramas en los hombros puros
De tu musa la túnica de nieve,
Yo concentro mis pétalos oscuros
Y soy el lirio de alabastro leve.

Para tu musa en rosa, me abro en rosa;
Mi corazón es miel, perfume y fuego,
Y vivo y muero de una sed gloriosa:
Tu sangre viva debe ser mi riego.

Cuando velada con un tul de luna
Bebe calma y azur en la laguna,
Yo soy el cisne que soñando vuela;

Y si en luto magnífico la vistes
Para vagar por los senderos tristes,
Soy la luz o la sombra de una estela . . .

To Your Muse

When you spill the gown of snow
Over the pure shoulders of your muse
I gather my dark petals
And I am the lily of light alabaster.

To your muse in rose, I open in rose;
My heart is honey, perfume, and fire;
And I live and die of a glorious thirst:
Your living blood should be water spilled on me.

When covered by a tulle of moonlight
It drinks calm and azure in the lake,
I am the swan that soars, dreaming;

And if in magnificent mourning you dress her
To wander along sad paths,
I am the light or the shadow of a stele . . .

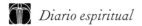 *Diario espiritual*

Es un lago mi alma;
Lago, vaso de cielo,
Nido de estrellas en la noche calma,
Copa del ave y de la flor, y suelo
De los cisnes y el alma.

—*Un lago fue mi alma . . .*—

Mi alma es una fuente
Donde canta un jardín; sonrosan rosas
Y vuelan alas en su melodía;
Engarza gemas armoniosamente
En el oro del día.

—*Mi alma fue una fuente . . .*—

Un arroyo es mi alma;
Larga caricia de cristal que rueda
Sobre carne de seda,
Camino de diamantes de la calma.

—*Fue un arroyo mi alma . . .*—

Mi alma es un torrente;
Como un manto de brillo y armonía,
Como un manto infinito desbordado
De una torre sombría,
¡Todo lo envuelve voluptuosamente!

De *Los astros del abismo* (1924) / 150

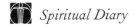 *Spiritual Diary*

My soul is a lake;
Lake, cup of heaven,
A nest of stars in the calm night,
A cup of the bird, and of the flower, and soil
Of swans and the soul.

    —My soul was a lake . . .—

My soul is a fountain
Where a garden sings; roses blush
And in its melody wings soar;
It sets gems harmoniously
In the gold of the day.

    —My soul was a fountain . . .—

A stream is my soul
A long caress of crystal that rolls
Upon silken flesh,
A path of diamonds of calm.

    —A stream was my soul . . .—

My soul is a torrent;
Like a shroud of brilliance and harmony,
Like an endless shroud overrun
By a gloomy tower,
Lustfully it swallows all!

From *The Stars of the Abyss* (1924) / 151

—Mi alma fue un torrente . . .—

Mi alma es todo un mar,
No un vómito siniestro del abismo:
Un palacio de perlas, con sirenas,
Abierto a todas las riberas buenas,
Y en que el amor divaga sin cesar . . .
Donde ni un lirio puede naufragar.

—Y mi alma fue mar . . .—

Mi alma es un fangal;
Llanto puso el dolor y tierra puso el mal.
Hoy apenas recuerda que ha sido de cristal;
No sabe de sirenas, de rosas ni armonía;
Nunca engarza una gema en el oro del día . . .
Llanto y llanto el dolor, y tierra y tierra el mal! . . .

Mi alma es un fangal;

¿Dónde encontrar el alma que en su entraña sombría
Prenda como una inmensa semilla de cristal?

De *Los astros del abismo* (1924) / 152

—My soul was a torrent . . .—

My soul is a whole sea,
Not a sinister vomit of the abyss:
A palace of pearls, with sirens,
Open to all good shores,
And where love wanders without end . . .
Where even a lily cannot drown.

—And my soul was a sea . . .—

My soul is a swamp;
Weeping placed the pain and earth placed the evil.
Today, it hardly remembers that it was crystal;
It knows not of sirens, roses or harmony;
It never sets a gem in the gold of the day . . .
Weeping and weeping the pain, and earth and earth the evil! . . .

My soul is a swamp;

Where to find the soul that in its dark bowels
Springs forth like an immense crystal seed?

La cita

En tu alcoba techada de ensueños, haz derroche
De flores y de luces de espíritu; mi alma,
Calzada de silencio y vestida de calma,
Irá a ti por la senda más negra de esta noche.

Apaga las bujías para ver cosas bellas;
Cierra todas las puertas para entrar la Ilusión;
Arranca del misterio un manojo de estrellas
Y enflora como un vaso triunfal tu corazón.

¡Y esperarás sonriendo, y esperarás llorando! . . .
Cuando llegue mi alma, tal vez reces pensando
Que el cielo dulcemente se derrama en tu pecho . . .

Para el amor divino ten un diván de calma,
O con el lirio místico que es su arma, mi alma
Apagará una a una las rosas de tu lecho!

 *The Encounter*

In your chamber covered with reverie, make waste
Of flowers and of spiritual lights; my soul,
Shod in silence and dressed in calm,
Will go after you down the darkest path of this night.

Turn out the lights and behold things beautiful;
Close all doors and enter illusion;
Uproot from mystery a handful of stars
And cover with flowers, like a triumphal vase, your heart.

And you will wait smiling, and you will wait weeping! . . .
When my soul arrives, perhaps you will pray, thinking
That heaven sweetly spills over your chest . . .

For divine love sit upon a sofa of calm,
Or with the mystical lily that is its sword, my soul
Will make vanish one by one the roses of your bed!

Anillo

Raro anillo que clarea,
Raro anillo que sombrea
Una profunda amatista,

Crepúsculo vespertino
Que en tu matinal platino
Engarzó espléndido artista.

El porvenir es de miedo . . .
¿Será tu destino un dedo
De tempestad o de calma?

Para clararte y sombrearte,
¡Si yo pudiera glisarte
En un dedo de mi alma! . . .

Ring

Rare ring that lightens
Rare ring that darkens
A deep amethyst,

A vesperian twilight
That in your matutinal platinum
A splendid artist mounted.

The future is made of fear
Will your destiny be a finger
Of tempest or of calm?

To lighten you or to darken you,
If I could only slide you
Over one finger of my soul! . . .

 *Serpentina*

En mis sueños de amor, ¡yo soy serpiente!
Gliso y ondulo como una corriente;
Dos píldoras de insomnio y de hipnotismo
   Son mis ojos; la punta de encanto
Es mi lengua . . . ¡y atraigo como el llanto!
   Soy un pomo de abismo.

Mi cuerpo es una cinta de delicia,
Glisa y ondula como una caricia . . .

Y en mis sueños de odio, ¡soy serpiente!
Mi lengua es una venenosa fuente;
Mi testa es la luzbélica diadema,
Haz de la muerte, en un fatal soslayo
Son mis pupilas; y mi cuerpo en gema
   ¡Es la vaina del rayo!

Si así sueño mi carne, así es mi mente:
   Un cuerpo largo, largo de serpiente,
Vibrando eterna, ¡voluptuosamente!

 *Serpentine*

In my dreams of love I am a serpent!
I glide and writhe like a stream;
Two capsules of insomnia and hypnosis
   Are my eyes; the point of enchantment
Is my tongue . . . and I beckon like a sob!
   I am a vial of the abyss.

My body is a ribbon of delight,
It glides and writhes like a caress . . .

And in my dreams of hate I am a serpent!
My tongue is a venomous fount;
My head is a diabolic diadem,
A beam of death, in a sidelong glance
Are my pupils; and my body in gem
   Is the sheath of a thunderbolt!

If thus I dream my flesh, my mind is this way;
   A long body, long, that of a serpent,
Vibrating eternally, voluptuously!

Sobre una tumba cándida

"Ha muerto . . . ha muerto" . . . dicen tan claro que no entiendo . . .
¡Verter licor tan suave en vaso tan tremendo! . . .
Tal vez fue un mal extraño tu mirar por divino,
Tu alma por celeste, o tu perfil por fino . . .

Tal vez fueron tus brazos dos capullos de alas . . .
¡Eran cielo a tu paso los jardines, las salas,
Y te asomaste al mundo dulce como una muerta!
Acaso tu ventana quedó una noche abierta,

—¡Oh, tentación de alas una ventana abierta!—

¡Y te sedujo un ángel por la estrella más pura . . .
Y tus alas abrieron, y cortaron la altura
En un tijereteo de luz y de candor!

Y en la alcoba que tu alma tapizaba de armiño,
Donde ardían los vasos de rosas de cariño,
La Soledad llamaba en silencio al Horror . . .

On a White Tomb

"She has died . . . she has died" . . . they say so clearly that I don't understand . . .
To spill so sweet a liquor into so terrible a cup! . . .
Perhaps your divine gaze was a strange illness,
Your heavenly soul, or your delicate profile . . .

Perhaps your arms were two blossoms of wings . . .
The gardens, the rooms, were heaven as you passed . . .
And you appeared to the world sweet, like a dead woman!
Perhaps your window remained open one night,

—Oh, temptation of wings, an open window!—

And through the purest star an angel seduced you . . .
And your wings opened, and cut the height
With a clipping of light and innocence!

And in the chamber that your soul covered with ermine,
Where the vases of roses of tenderness burned,
In silence, loneliness was calling to horror . . .

Mi plinto

Es creciente, diríase
 Que tiene una infinita raíz ultraterrena . . .
Lábranlo muchas manos
Retorcidas y negras,
Con muchas piedras vivas . . .
Muchas oscuras piedras
Crecientes como larvas.

Como al impulso de una omnipotente araña
Las piedras crecen, crecen;
Las manos labran, labran,

 —Labrad, labrad, ¡oh, manos!
 Creced, creced, ¡oh, piedras!
 Ya me embriaga un glorioso
 Aliento de palmeras.

Ocultas entre el pliegue más negro de la noche,
Debajo del rosal más florido del alba,
Tras el bucle más rubio de la tarde,
Las tenebrosas larvas
De piedra crecen, crecen,
Las manos labran, labran,
Como capullos negros
De infernales arañas.

 —Labrad, labrad, ¡oh, manos!
 Creced, creced, ¡oh, piedras!
 Ya me abrazan los brazos
 De viento de la sierra.

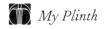 *My Plinth*

It is rising, one would say
  That it has an endless unearthly root . . .
It is built by many hands
Twisted and black,
With many living stones . . .
Many obscure stones
Rising like larvae.

As to the impulse of an omnipotent spider
The stones rise, rise;
The hands build, build,

  —Build, build, O, hands!
  Rise, rise, O, stones!
  A glorious breath of palm trees
  Already intoxicates me.

Hidden in the darkest fold of the night,
Beneath the most flowery rosebush of dawn,
Behind the most golden lock of dusk,
The dark larvae
Of stone rise, rise
The hands build, build
Like black rose buds
Of infernal spiders.

  Build, build, O, hands!
  Rise, rise, O, stones!
  The arms of the mountain wind
  Already embrace me.

Van entrando los soles en la alcoba nocturna,
Van abriendo las lunas el carmín de nácar . . .

Tenaces como ebrias
De un veneno de araña
Las piedras crecen, crecen,
Las manos labran, labran.

—Labrad, labrad, ¡oh, manos!
Creced, creced, ¡oh, piedras!
¡Ya siento una celeste
Serenidad de estrella!

The suns of the nocturnal chamber are entering,
The moons are opening the carmine of pearl . . .

Tenacious as if inebriated
From a spider's poison
The stones rise, rise,
The hands build, build

—Build, build, O, hands!
Rise, rise, O, stones!
I already feel the heavenly
Serenity of a star!

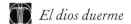 *El dios duerme*

A Julieta, sobre la tumba de Julio.

El dios duerme su gloria a tu amparo, Julieta;
Una lanza de amor en tu brazo sonrosa;
Su *berceuse* fue blanca, tu *berceuse* es violeta . . .
Eras rosa en su lecho, eres lirio en su fosa.

—Las serpientes del mundo, apuntadas, acechan
Las palomas celestes que en tu carne sospechan.—

El dios duerme, Julieta; su almohada es de estrellas
Pulidas por tu mano, y tu sombra es su manto;
La veladora insomne de tu mirada estrellas
En la Noche, rival única de tu encanto.

—Y las bellas serpientes, encendidas, meditan
En las suaves palomas que en tu cuerpo dormitan.—

Y el dios despertará nadie sabe en qué día,
Nadie sueña en qué tierra de glorificación.
Si se durmió llorando, que al despertar sonría . . .
En el vaso de luna de tu melancolía
Salva como un diamante rosa tu corazón.

¡Y sálvalo de Todo sobre tu corazón!

De *Los astros del abismo* (1924) / 166

 *The God Sleeps*

To Julieta, over the grave of Julio.

The god sleeps in his glory under your protection, Julieta;
A spear of love blushes in your arm;
His berceuse was white, your berceuse is purple . . .
You were a rose in his bed, you are a lily on his grave.

—The serpents of the world, pointed, spy upon
The suspecting celestial doves in your flesh.—

The god sleeps, Julieta; his pillow is made of stars
Polished by your hand, and your shadow is his robe;
The sleepless watch of your star-gazing
In the night, sole rival of your charm.

—And the beautiful serpents, inflamed, meditate
On the soft doves that sleep upon your body.—

And the god will awake, no one knows what day,
No one dreams in what land of glorification.
If he fell asleep crying, may he smile upon awakening . . .
In the moon-white vase of your melancholy
Rescue, like a pink diamond, your heart.

And rescue him from everything upon your heart!

Julio Herrera y Reissig (1875–1910) was another great poet of the Uruguayan
modernismo, of the same generation as Delmira Agustini. Julieta de la Fuente
was Herrera y Reissig's wife, whom he married on July 22, 1908, two years before
his death.

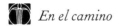 *En el camino*

Yo iba sola al Misterio bajo un sol de locura,
Y tú me derramaste tu sombra, peregrino;
Tu mirada fue buena como una senda oscura,
Como una senda húmeda que vendara el camino.

Me fue pródiga y fértil tu alforja de ternura:
Tuve el candor del pan, y la llama del vino;
Mas tu alma en un pliegue de su astral vestidura,
Abrojo de oro y sombra se llevó mi destino.

Mis manos, que tus manos abrigaron, ya nunca
Se enfriarán, y guardando la dulce malla trunca
De tus caricias ¡nunca podrán acariciar! . . .

En mi cuerpo, una torre de recuerdo y espera
Que se siente de mármol y se sueña de cera,
Tu Sombra logra rosas de fuego en el hogar;
Y en mi alma, un castillo desolado y sonoro
Con pátinas de tedio y humedades de lloro,

¡Tu sombra logra rosas de nieve en el hogar!

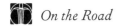 *On the Road*

I went along, alone, to the mystery beneath a sun of madness,
And you spilled your shadow upon me, pilgrim;
Your glance was kind, like a dark path,
Like a damp path covering the way.

Prodigal and fertile to me was your bag of tenderness:
I had the simplicity of bread, and the flame of wine;
But your soul in a fold of its astral raiment,
A burr of gold and shadow, bore off my destiny.

My hands, which your hands covered, never
Shall grow cold, and holding fast in the sweet close mesh
Of your caress, will never be able to caress! . . .

In my body, a tower of memory and hope
With the feel of marble and the dream of wax,
Your shadow casts roses of fire in the hearth
And in my soul, a castle desolate and sounding
With patinas of tedium and moistness of tears,

Your shadow casts roses of snow in the hearth!

 *Boca a boca*

Copa de vida donde quiero y sueño
Beber la muerte con fruición sombría,
Surco de fuego donde logra Ensueño
Fuertes semillas de melancolía.

Boca que besas a distancia y llamas
En silencio, pastilla de locura
Color de sed y húmeda de llamas . . .
¡Verja de abismos es tu dentadura!

Sexo de un alma triste de gloriosa,
El placer unges de dolor; tu beso,
Puñal de fuego en vaina de embeleso,
Me come en sueños como un cáncer rosa . . .

Joya de sangre y luna, vaso pleno
De rosas de silencio y de armonía,
Nectario de su miel y su veneno,
Vampiro vuelto mariposa al día.

Tijera ardiente de glaciales lirios,
Panal de besos, ánfora viviente
Donde brindan delicias y delirios
Fresas de aurora en vino de Poniente . . .

Estuche de encendidos terciopelos
En que su voz es fúlgida presea,
Alas del verbo amenazando vuelos,
Cáliz en donde el corazón flamea.

De *Los astros del abismo* (1924) / 170

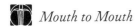 *Mouth to Mouth*

Cup of life where I love and dream
Of drinking death with somber satisfaction,
Furrow of fire where fantasy creates
Bold seeds of melancholy.

O mouth, you kiss from a distance, and beckon
In silence, a tablet of madness
The color of thirst and humid with flames . . .
Your teeth are a gate to the abyss!

Sex of a sad soul of glory
You anoint pleasure with pain; your kiss,
A dagger of fire in a sheath of ecstasy,
It devours me in dreams like a pink cancer . . .

A jewel of blood and moonlight; a vase filled
With roses of silence and harmony,
Nectary of his honey and his poison,
A vampire turned butterfly by daylight.

Ardent knife of glacial lilies,
Honeycomb of kisses, a living amphora
Where berries of dawn in the wine of dusk
Offer deliria and delight . . .

A case of flaming velvets
In which his voice is shining prey,
Wings of the word threatening flight
Chalice where the heart blazes.

Pico rojo del buitre del deseo
Que hubiste sangre y alma entre mi boca,
De tu largo y sonante picoteo
Brotón una llaga como flor de roca.
Inaccesible . . . Si otra vez mi vida
Cruzas, dando a la tierra removida
Siembra de oro tu verbo fecundo,
Tu curarás la misteriosa herida:
Lirio de muerte, cóndor de vida,
¡Flor de tu beso que perfuma al mundo!

Red beak of the vulture of desire
Whose blood and soul were inside my mouth,
From your long and sounding strike
A wound sprung up like a flower from a rock.

Inaccessible . . . If another time you cross my life
Sowing the golden earth with your fertile word,
You will heal the mysterious wound:
Lily of death, condor of life,
Flower of your kiss that perfumes the world!

Selene

Medallón de la noche con la imagen del día
Y herido por la perla de la melancolía;
Hogar de los espíritus, corazón del azul,
La tristeza de novia en su torre de tul;
Máscara del misterio o de la soledad,
Clavada como un hongo sobre la inmensidad;
Primer sueño del mundo, florecido en el cielo,
O la primer blasfemia suspendida en su vuelo . . .
Gran lirio astralizado, copa de luz y niebla,
Caricia o quemadura del sol en la tiniebla;
Bruja eléctrica y pálida que orienta en los caminos,
Extravía en las almas, hipnotiza destinos . . .
Desposada del mundo en magnética ronda;
Sonámbula celeste paso a paso de blonda;
Patria blanca o siniestra de lirios o de cirios,
Oblea de pureza, pastilla de delirios;
Talismán del abismo, melancólico y fuerte,
Imantado de vida, imantado de muerte . . .
A veces me pareces una tumba sin dueño . . .
Y a veces . . . una cuna ¡toda blanca! tendida
       [de esperanza y de ensueño . . .

Selene

Medallion of the night with the image of the day
And wounded by the pearl of melancholy;
Home of the spirits, heart of the azure,
The sadness of a bride in her tower of tulle;
Mask of mystery or solitude,
Clinging like a mushroom upon immensity;
First dream of the world, blooming in the sky,
Or the first blasphemy hanging in its flight . . .
A great astral lily, a cup of light and mist,
A caress or sunburn in the darkness,
An electric and pale witch that guides on paths,
Misleads souls, hypnotizes destinies . . .
Spouse of the world in your magnetic rounds;
Heavenly somnambulist step by step to light;
White or sinister home of lilies or candles,
Medal of purity, pill of delirium;
Talisman of the abyss, strong and melancholic,
Magnetized by life, magnetized by death . . .
Sometimes you seem like grave without a master
And sometimes . . . a cradle, all white! filled with
          [hope and fantasy . . .

Tus ojos, esclavos moros

En tu frialdad se emboscaban
Los grandes esclavos moros;
Negros y brillando en oros
De lejos me custodiaban.

Y, devorantes, soñaban
En mí no sé qué tesoros . . .
Tras el cristal de los lloros
Guardaban y amenazaban.

Ritmaban alas angélicas,
Ritmaban manos luzbélicas
Sus dos pantallas extrañas;

Y al yo mirarlos por juego,
Sus alabardas de fuego
Llegaron a mis entrañas.

Your Eyes, Moorish Slaves

In your coldness were ensconced
The great Moorish slaves;
Dark and shining in golds
From a distance they guarded me.

And, devouring, they dreamt
In me, I know not what treasures . . .
Behind the crystal of tears
They guarded and threatened.

They beat angelic wings,
They pounded satanic hands,
Their two strange screens;

And when I looked upon them coquettishly,
Their fiery halberds
Pierced my entrails.

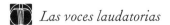 *Las voces laudatorias*

Para Andrés

Hermano: a veces dudo si existes o te sueño;
Coronado de espíritus reinas en la Belleza
Teniendo por vasallos la Vida y el Ensueño,
Y por novia la Gloria que el crepúsculo reza:

"Dios salve de sus ojos los dos largos estíos;
"Y mariposa ebria de sol, su cabellera;
"Y su boca, una rosa fresca sobre los ríos
"Del Fuego y la Armonía; y los vasos de cera

"De sus manos colmadas de rosas de cariño;
"Y su cuerpo sin sombra que reviste un armiño
"De castidad sobre una púrpura de pasión;

"Y, ante todo, Dios salve el rincón de su vida
"Do el Espíritu Santo de su espíritu anida:
"Ante todo, Dios salve en mí su corazón!"

El Ensueño se encierra en su boca sedeña,
El Ensueño no habla ni nada: sueña, sueña . . .

Y la Vida cantando a la sombra de un lloro:
"Su mirada me viste de terciopelo y fuego,
"O me vierte dos copas de tiniebla y de oro
"O abre en rosas mi carne con un cálido riego:

"Su cuerpo hecho de pétalos de placer y de encanto,
"Corola el cáliz negro de la melancolía,
"Y su espíritu vuela de sus labios en canto
"En un pájaro rosa con un ala sombría.

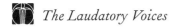 *The Laudatory Voices*

To Andrés

Brother: at times I doubt if you exist or I dream you;
Crowned by spirits you reign in beauty
Having as servants life and fantasy,
And for your bride the glory that dusk utters:

"May God rescue from his eyes the two long summers;
"And his hair, a butterfly inebriated by sun;
"And his mouth, a fresh rose upon the rivers
"Of fire and harmony; and the wax vases

"Of his hands, showered with roses of tenderness
"And his shadowless body adorned in ermine
"With chastity over a purple of passion;

"And, above all, may God save the corner of his life
"Where the Holy Ghost of his spirit lives:
"Above all, May God save his heart in me!"

Illusion is sealed in his silky mouth,
Illusion speaks not a word: it dreams and dreams . . .

And life singing under the shadow of a cry:
"His gaze dresses me with velvet and fire,
"Or spills on me two cups of darkness and gold
"Or it opens my flesh in roses with a warm sprinkle:

"His body made of petals of pleasure and charm,
"Forms the corolla around the dark calyx of melancholy,
"And his spirit soars from his lips singing
"In a rosy bird with a somber wing.

From *The Stars of the Abyss* (1924) / 179

"Cuando clava el divino monstruo de su belleza
"Su dentadura húmeda de miel y de tristeza,
"Es un mal o es un bien tan extraño y tan fuerte,

"Que la cabeza cae como una piedra oscura
"Buscando la fantástica venda de la locura
"O una honda y narcótica almohada de muerte".

Y el ensueño se encierra en su boca sedeña;
El ensueño no habla ni nada: sueña, sueña . . .

Y yo te digo: hermano del corazón sonoro,
A tu paso los muros dan ventanas de anhelo,
Y se enjoyan las almas de sonrisa y de lloro
Y arde una bienvenida de rosas en el suelo.

En tu lira de brazos que abrazaran el vuelo
Fulgen las siete llaves de lírico tesoro,
O los siete peldaños de una escala de oro
Que asciende del abismo y desciende del cielo.

¡Eres Francia! . . . Tu sangre, tu alma, tu poesía
Forman un lis de fuego, de gloria y de armonía
Con que París corona su frente de crisol;

Si un día la nostalgia te diera fiebre o frío
Deja fluir tu espíritu como un Sena sombrío
O ábrelo como un manto de tu lejano sol!

Y el ensueño encerrado en su boca sedeña;
El Ensueño no habla ni nada: sueña, sueña . . .

"When it fixes the divine monster of his beauty
"His smile humid with honey and sadness,
"It is something bad or good so strange and strong,

"That the head falls like a dark stone
"Looking for the fantastic bandage of madness
"Or a deep and narcotic pillow of death."

And illusion is sealed in his silky mouth,
Illusion speaks not a word: it dreams and dreams . . .

And I tell you: brother of the sonorous heart,
When you appear, walls give windows of longing,
And souls are adorned with smiles and sobs
And there flames a welcome of roses on the ground.

In the lyre of your arms that embraced the flight
Shine the seven keys of a lyric treasure,
Or the seven steps of a golden scale
That ascends from the abyss and descends from Heaven.

You are France! . . . Your blood, your soul, your poetry
Form a lily of fire, glory and harmony
With which Paris crowns the crucible of her brow;

If one day nostalgia should bring you fever or chill
Let your spirit flow like a somber Seine
Or open it like a cloak of your distant sun!

And illusion is sealed in his silky mouth,
Illusion speaks not a word: it dreams and dreams . . .

 *El rosario de Eros*

CUENTAS DE MÁRMOL

Yo, la estatua de mármol con cabeza de fuego,
Apagando mis sienes en frío y blanco ruego . . .

Engarzad en un gesto de palmera o de astro
Vuestro cuerpo, esa hipnótica alhaja de alabastro
Tallada a besos puros y bruñida en la edad;
Sereno, tal habiendo la luna por coraza;
Blanco, más que si fuerais la espuma de la Raza,
Y desde el tabernáculo de vuestra castidad,
Elevad a mí los lises hondos de vuestra alma;
Mi sombra besará vuestro manto de calma,
Que creciendo, creciendo me envolverá con Vos;
Luego será mi carne en la vuestra perdida . . .
Luego será mi alma en la vuestra diluída . . .
Luego será la gloria . . . y seremos un dios!

—Amor de blanco y frío,
Amor de estatuas, lirios, astros, dioses . . .
¡Tú me lo des, Dios mío!

De *Los astros del abismo* (1924) / 182

 *The Rosary of Eros*

BEADS OF MARBLE

I, the marble statue with a head of fire,
Cooling my temples in cold and white prayer . . .

In a gesture of palm or of the star
Affix your body, that hypnotic jewel of alabaster
Sculpted with pure kisses and burnished by age;
Serene, like having the moon as a cuirass;
White, more than if you were the foam of race,
And from the tabernacle of your chastity,
Raise to me the deep lilies of your soul;
My shadow will kiss your shroud of calm,
Which rising, rising will enwrap me with you;
Then my flesh will be lost in yours . . .
Then my soul will be diluted in yours . . .
Then there will be glory . . . and we will be a god!

—Love of white and cold,
Love of statues, lilies, stars, gods . . .
Give him to me, my God!

Los lechos negros logran la más fuerte
Rosa de amor; arraigan en la muerte.

Grandes lechos tendidos de tristeza,
Tallados a puñal y doselados
De insomnio; las abiertas
Cortinas dicen cabelleras muertas;
Buenas como cabezas
Hermanas son las hondas almohadas:
Plintos del Sueño y del Misterio gradas.

Si así en un lecho como flor de muerte,
Damos llorando, como un fruto fuerte
Maduro de pasión, en carnes y almas,
Serán especies desoladas, bellas,
Que besen el perfil de las estrellas
Pisando los cabellos de las palmas!

—Gloria al amor sombrío,
Como la Muerte pudre y ennoblece
¡Tú me lo des, Dios mío!

BEADS OF SHADOW

Darkened beds fetch the strongest
Rose of love, they root in death.

Magnificent beds spread with sadness
Sculpted with a dagger and canopied
By insomnia; the open
Curtains tell of lifeless heads of hair;
Good like heads
Sisters are the thick pillows:
Plinths of reverie and stairs of mystery.

If thus in a bed like a flower of death,
We give, crying, like a strong fruit
Ripened with passion, in flesh and souls,
They will be desolate, beautiful species,
That may kiss the profile of the stars
Treading upon the locks of the palms!

—Glory to the somber love,
Like death it rots and ennobles
Give him to me, my God!

Cerrar la puerta cómplice con rumor de caricia,
Deshojar hacia el mal el lirio de una veste . . .
—La seda es un pecado, el desnudo es celeste;
Y es un cuerpo mullido un diván de delicia.—

Abrir brazos . . . así todo ser es alado,
O una cálida lira dulcemente rendida
De canto y de silencio . . . más tarde, en el helado
Más allá de un espejo como un lago inclinado,
Ver la olímpica bestia que elabora la vida . . .

Amor rojo, amor mío;
Sangre de mundos y rubor de cielos . . .
¡Tú me lo des, Dios mío!

BEADS OF FIRE

To close the complicit door with a murmur of a caress,
To shed down to evil the lily of a dress . . .
—Silk is a sin, nakedness is heavenly;
And a soft body is a bed of delight.—

To open arms . . . thus all beings are wingèd,
Or a warm lyre sweetly rendered
In song and in silence . . . later, in the frozen
Hereafter of a mirror like a tilted lake,
To see the Olympic beast that fashions life . . .

Red love, love of mine;
Blood of worlds, and blush of skies . . .
Give him to me, my God!

Lejos como en la muerte
Siento arder una vida vuelta siempre hacia mí,
Fuego lento hecho de ojos insomnes, más que fuerte
Si de su allá insondable dora todo mi aquí.
Sobre tierras y mares su horizonte es mi ceño,
Como un cisne sonámbulo duerme sobre mi sueño
Y es su paso velado de distancia y reproche
El seguimiento dulce de los perros sin dueño
Que han roído ya el hambre, la tristeza y la noche
Y arrastran su cadena de misterio y ensueño.

Amor de luz, un río
Que es el camino de cristal del Bien.
¡Tú me lo des, Dios mío!

De *Los astros del abismo* (1924) / 188

BEADS OF LIGHT

Far away as if in death
I feel burning a life turned always towards me,
Slow flame made of sleepless eyes, more than strong
If from its bottomless hereafter it gilds all my here and now.
Upon lands and seas its horizon is my frown,
Like a somnambulist swan it sleeps upon my dream
And its veiled step of distance and reproach is
The sweet pursuit of masterless hounds
That already have gnawed upon hunger, sorrow and night
And drag their chain of mystery and illusion.

Love of light, a river
That is the crystal path of goodness.
Give him to me, my God!

Los cuervos negros sufren hambre de carne rosa;
En engañosa luna mi escultura reflejo,
Ellos rompen sus picos, martillando el espejo,
Y al alejarme irónica, intocada y gloriosa,
Los cuervos negros vuelan hartos de carne rosa.

Amor de burla y frío
Mármol que el tedio barnizó de fuego
O lirio que el rubor vistió de rosa,
Siempre lo dé, Dios mío . . .

O rosario fecundo,
Collar vivo que encierra
La garganta del mundo.

Cadena de la tierra
Constelación caída.

O rosario imantado de serpientes,
Glisa hasta el fin entre mis dedos sabios,
Que en tu sonrisa de cincuenta dientes
Con un gran beso se prendió mi vida:
Una rosa de labios.

FALSE BEADS

The black ravens suffer hunger for pink flesh;
In deceptive moonlight I reflect my sculpture,
They break their beaks, hammering the mirror,
And when walking away, ironic, untouched and glorious,
The black ravens fly, glutted with pink flesh.

Love of mockery and cold
Marble that tedium varnished with fire
O lily that blush adorned with rose,
May you always grant it, my God . . .

O fertile rosary,
Living necklace that encircles
The throat of the world.

Chain of land
Fallen constellation.

O rosary magnetized with serpents,
Slither till the end of time between my wise fingers,
That in your smile of fifty teeth
With a great kiss my life ignited:
A rose of lips.

Alejandro Cáceres is an associate professor of Spanish in the Department of Foreign Languages and Literatures at Southern Illinois University Carbondale and a member of the Academia Uruguaya de Letras. Born in Montevideo, Uruguay, he has lived in the United States since 1977. His research on Agustini, ongoing since the early 1980s, has resulted in the publication of several articles; lectures at both the Library of Congress and the National Library of Uruguay; and, in 1999, a critical edition of Agustini's complete poetry, in Spanish, which also included the most comprehensive study of criticism written on the poet. The present volume constitutes the most comprehensive collection on Delmira Agustini ever published in English.